Thriving as a Supply, Substitute or Cover Teacher

Supply or substitute educators play a crucial role in keeping classrooms running and student learning on track. However, stepping into an unfamiliar classroom, with students you've never met and minimal guidance, is far more challenging than it may seem. Drawing on over 20 years of classroom and leadership experience, this practical guide explores how temporary teachers can navigate the complex world of unfamiliar schools, build meaningful connections with students and develop a strong professional identity.

Each chapter is designed to support you in managing the unique demands of being a temporary teacher. You'll learn how to maintain high expectations, manage behaviour, build credibility and create meaningful learning opportunities, even under pressure. Throughout there are real-life stories and examples from temporary teachers around the world, and expert insights from current teachers and school leaders to illustrate how the ideas in the book can be applied in different contexts.

More than a handbook for cover work, this book is a toolkit for professional growth, confidence and belonging. Whether you're aiming for permanent roles or excelling in temporary positions, it will empower you to see yourself as a skilled professional, make a lasting impact on students and rediscover your sense of purpose in the classroom.

Richard Wheadon has over 20 years' teaching experience and currently supports 10 secondary schools as a school improvement partner. He previously spent time as a supply teacher, which gave him the flexibility to write his first book, *Learning Habits*. He is a Chartered College of Teaching Fellow and has presented at conferences internationally.

A great combination of scientifically backed research paired with real world knowledge written by current and former supply teachers who have been there and done that. Accessible and exciting, this is a great read for substitute teachers interested in taking their skills to the next level.

Jim Steward Allen, *Substitute Teacher*

I enjoyed the whole book but the last chapter focused on wellbeing I will take forward, not just in my supply teaching, but in life in general.

Mrs Walsh, *Primary Supply Teacher*

Leaving the classroom after 29 years, this is a practical, accessible toolkit for me as I continue my new role as a cover teacher. Each chapter is packed with adaptable examples, usable in any lesson, across subjects, boosting my confidence to be able to create those meaningful learning opportunities.

Caroline Webster, *Secondary Cover Teacher*

Thriving as a Supply, Substitute or Cover Teacher

Confident, Impactful and More Than Temporary

Richard Wheadon

Routledge
Taylor & Francis Group
LONDON AND NEW YORK

Designed cover image: © Getty Images

First published 2027
by Routledge
4 Park Square, Milton Park, Abingdon, Oxon OX14 4RN

and by Routledge
605 Third Avenue, New York, NY 10158

Routledge is an imprint of the Taylor & Francis Group, an informa business

British Library Cataloguing-in-Publication Data
A catalogue record for this book is available from the British Library

ISBN: 978-1-041-31722-7 (hbk)
ISBN: 978-1-041-31721-0 (pbk)
ISBN: 978-1-003-78041-0 (ebk)

DOI: 10.4324/9781003780410

Typeset in Melior
by SPi Technologies India Pvt Ltd (Straive)

Contents

UK and US Terms: A Quick Guide for Temporary Teachers

This book is written for supply teachers in the United Kingdom, substitute teachers in the United States, and temporary educators around the world. Most of the language you'll see reflects the UK system, but I know many of you will be reading from across the pond—or beyond! This glossary is here to make things easier, helping you understand the UK terms and their closest US equivalents, so you can follow along, apply the strategies and feel confident no matter where you're teaching. Think of it as your little survival guide to the vocabulary used throughout the book.

UK Term	Definition (UK)	US Counterpart / Explanation
Supply teacher	A teacher who works on a temporary basis, often covering for absent permanent teachers.	Substitute teacher or 'sub'
Cover supervisor	Member of staff who supervises a class during a teacher's absence, but often work in one school.	Building sub
Senior leadership	The group of school leaders responsible for strategic decisions.	School administration or administrative team
Seating plan	A diagram or chart showing where students sit in the classroom.	Seating chart
Behaviour policy	A school-wide set of rules and procedures for managing student behaviour.	Student conduct policy or discipline policy
DfE (Department for Education)	The UK government department responsible for education policy and standards.	Department of Education (federal) or State Department of Education (state-level authority)

(Continued)

UK Term	Definition (UK)	US Counterpart / Explanation
Teacher Training	UK programmes that qualify someone to teach	Teacher preparation programs
Safeguarding	Policies and procedures to protect children from abuse, neglect or harm, including reporting and prevention responsibilities.	Child protection; often referred to as 'mandated reporting' and school safety protocols
SEN (special educational needs)	A legal term for students who require additional support due to learning difficulties, disabilities or other barriers to learning.	Special education (SPED); refers to students with Individualized Education Programs (IEPs)
EHCP (Education, Health, and Care Plan)	A legal plan for a child or young person with significant special educational needs, outlining the support they should receive.	Individualized Education Program (IEP); a formal plan detailing special education support, accommodations and goals
PP Pupil Premium	Additional funding provided to publicly funded UK schools to support disadvantaged pupils, aiming to close the attainment gap.	Title I funding or disadvantaged student support programs; funding provided to schools to support students from low-income families

Preface

'It's just supply teaching, I'll be fine'.

A phrase I'll never forget. It was my confident response to my agent in our first meeting before I took up my first supply post.

After 20 years in the classroom, the last 10 as a senior leader, I decided to make a change. I left school leadership to write a book about education. The idea had started back in 2023 when, as a senior leader, I found myself facing a problem I couldn't solve. Despite giving students a consistent, evidence-informed diet of teaching, I was still disappointed by some of their outcomes.

It turned out that even with 'good' teaching, students can still make poor decisions once they leave the classroom. That realisation sent me down a new path. I began researching what really drives learning behaviour and how students can make better choices. Eventually, that journey led to my first book, *Learning Habits*.

At the time, I told myself I had only one book in me. It felt like *Learning Habits* was the result of 20 years of experience and reflection, and I didn't think I had anything left to say.

While I was writing the book, I decided to take on some supply work. It was, at first, a financial decision. I thought it might help me extend the time I could stay out of senior leadership so that I could finish and promote the book properly. What I didn't realise then was that supply teaching would end up inspiring a second book.

I became a teacher, like so many others, to make a positive difference in young people's lives. I'm the product of a teacher who believed in me. My physics teacher, Mr Coombes, saw something I didn't see in myself. By the age of 25, only a few years into the job, I'd achieved everything I had ever imagined I could. Having never really expected to make it as a teacher, I started to look for new challenges. I wanted to have a bigger impact, so I went into leadership, eventually becoming an assistant headteacher leading teaching and learning at a large secondary school.

After that, I began to wonder what else I could do to make a difference. I started speaking at conferences across the UK, and later internationally, and I began writing about my work. My goal was always the same: To help students, whether directly or by supporting teachers who could then do the same for their own pupils. That is, ultimately, what led to this second book.

'It's just supply teaching, I'll be fine'.

But I wasn't.

It's often said in staffrooms that people change when they become senior leaders, and I now understand why. As a classroom teacher, your main focus is on your students. As a senior leader, the noise comes from every direction – parents, teachers, governors, external regulatory bodies like Ofsted in the UK and many other sources. It becomes harder to always put students first, even when you want to. You also become removed from the daily rhythm of teaching five lessons a day, and you start to rely more on your position than on your practice.

On my first day of supply, I arrived at school far too early. I was nervous and wanted to be as prepared as possible. In fact, I was so early that the person meant to greet me wasn't even in school yet. A member of the office staff, who had only just started her shift, eventually arrived. She handed me a few documents I barely had time to read before taking me to the classroom. On the way, she explained how to use the call-out system if I needed to remove any students.

I smiled and said, 'Don't worry, I'll be fine'.

Looking back, that confidence was really arrogance. It showed how many blind spots I'd developed after years in leadership.

A few minutes later, the Head of Science appeared with a USB stick. 'All the lessons are on here', he said. The admin assistant turned to him and added, 'We don't have a laptop for him'.

At that moment, panic set in. As they both disappeared to find a solution, I stood alone in an unfamiliar classroom, surrounded by silence and my own thoughts. I remember thinking, *What have I done?*

Seconds before the bell rang, a laptop finally arrived. I loaded up the PowerPoint, which contained a few slides and some questions. I took a deep breath and went to the door to greet the students, smiling and saying hello to each one as they entered. Hardly any replied.

I won't go into too much detail about that first lesson, but let's just say it was far from smooth. I ended up removing two students and I'm fairly sure I didn't follow the correct policy. I was completely overwhelmed, a textbook case of cognitive overload.

'It's just supply teaching, I'll be fine'.

On any given day in the UK, around 18,000 supply teachers are working in schools. Many secondary schools also employ one or two full-time cover teachers to manage absence. In the United States, there are thought to be around 400,000 substitute teachers, rising to over a million for longer-term positions.

And that's when it hit me. I had found my second book.

A rough calculation suggests that in the UK, around 2.5 million students are taught by a temporary teacher every single day. In the United States, that number exceeds 30 million. During my first 12 weeks of supply, I taught classes that included more than half of the students in one school.

I realised that my 20 years of experience could be used for a new purpose. I wanted to support supply teachers, to help them make a real difference to the students in front of them. Because it isn't *just* supply teaching. It requires a unique set of skills, thoughtful preparation and a deep understanding of how learning happens.

If *Learning Habits* was about how students learn, this book is about how teachers, especially those stepping into unfamiliar classrooms, can create the conditions for that learning to happen. It began with the words, 'It's just supply teaching', but as I soon discovered, it's anything but.

Introduction

I have been an educator for over 20 years, teaching students in inner-city London and Liverpool. I have led three science faculties, taken responsibility for the quality of education across entire schools, spoken at conferences in the UK and abroad, written a book called *Learning Habits* and now work with schools around the world to help them develop teaching and learning. I don't share these experiences to boast – I share them to highlight a fact that may surprise some but perhaps not the main audience of this book: The hardest role I have ever had in education is supply teaching.

Recently, a discussion appeared in a Facebook group for supply teachers: *If you had to write a book about your experience of supply teaching, what would it be called?* The responses were revealing.

Some focused on the lack of respect from students:

- 'Wait, you're a real teacher?'
- 'Yes, we have supply'.
- 'Yay, we have a sub'.
- 'Are you a proper teacher?'
- 'Did you ever have a real class?'

Others highlighted the isolation of the role:

- 'The Invisible Teacher'
- 'The Undervalued'
- 'Indispensable, Expendable'
- 'Five Years of Loneliness'

DOI: 10.4324/9781003780410-1

Many referenced the daily challenges of dealing with students:

- 'The Class from Hell: Tales from the Frontline'
- 'You Swallowed What?'
- 'This Is Your Third Reminder'

Some poked fun at the repetitive or bureaucratic grind of the role:

- 'Have You Got Your DBS?'
- 'What's Your Name Again?'
- 'Is There a Login I Can Use?'
- 'Scream Season 87' – presumably referring to cover work left for a class that feels pointless.

But my favourites, which I think encapsulate the role perfectly, are:

- 'Magic, Mayhem, and No Meetings' – these words capture the essence of supply teaching: A mix of unpredictability, humour, challenge and resilience.
- 'I Did My Best with the Tools I Was Given' – this book is an attempt to provide the tools and strategies to support teachers, helping them manage the day-to-day realities of supply work and build confidence to not just survive, but thrive.

Supply teaching can feel overwhelming, unpredictable and isolating. Yet within these challenges lies an opportunity – to reflect, to adapt and to develop practices that make a real difference in the classroom. This book is a guide to navigating that world – from the first-day fundamentals to the strategies and techniques that allow you to teach with purpose and confidence, wherever you are.

1.1 Who Is This Book For?

Across the world, there are many different names for temporary teachers – and this alone can create confusion about the roles and responsibilities of this large and diverse group of educators.

In the UK, *supply teacher* is the general term used for qualified teachers who cover for staff who are absent. Alongside them are *cover supervisors* (sometimes called cover teachers), who may have experience working with children or in school settings but often do not hold formal teaching qualifications.

In the United States, these distinctions are less clearly defined. The term *substitute teacher* is used for all temporary teaching staff, regardless of qualification, although the term *guest teacher* has started to be used, perhaps in an attempt to reduce some of the stigma attached to substitute teaching. It's more common for substitutes not to hold formal teaching credentials, although many states and districts expect some form of professional development or certification. Some substitutes – known as *building subs* – work consistently in the same school, functioning much like a UK cover supervisor.

My exploration of the sector has shown that many qualified teachers in the United States have chosen to work as substitutes for a variety of personal and professional reasons. Equally, many educators begin their journey in education as substitutes before deciding to pursue full teacher certification.

For the remainder of this book, I will use the term *temporary teacher* to encompass the wide range of roles this text is intended to support. Whether you are brand new to the teaching profession, working across multiple schools or based in a single school covering for different members of staff, the term *temporary teacher* applies. It refers to any teacher who holds temporary responsibility for the learning of the students in their care.

I.2 Finding Your Way

Like some who will pick up this book, I struggled to secure a teaching position at the start of my career. I entered the profession at 21, bright-eyed and very naive. My training year didn't go according to plan – there were many ups and downs. After completing my degree, I moved to Cheshire for my teacher training with my partner, now wife, in the area where she grew up. Despite several interviews, I wasn't able to secure a position. I still remember how nervous I was during interviews – I couldn't even make eye contact.

After settling in Cheshire and making new friends, it became clear that I would have to move to a bigger city to find work. We chose London, inspired by my teacher training mentor, who had made a similar move. I share this story to offer hope to those looking for permanent work. After several rejections, the move to London marked the start of a career I am proud of.

When I began writing this book, I reached out to a variety of educators recognised as experts in the field. Many have deep knowledge of pedagogy (the science and craft of teaching) and have authored their own books. Throughout this book, you will read case studies from these educators, sharing their expertise to support temporary teachers. What surprised me most was how many recognised experts, like myself, started their careers on shaky ground. Many began by taking temporary roles to develop their skills.

To finish this introduction, I want to share a case study. A good friend of mine, Adam Kohlbeck, is Director of Teaching Quality at Chiltern Learning Trust, co-host of the educational podcast *Edupulse*, currently studying for his PhD, and co-author of the books *Adaptive Expertise* and *Succeeding as a Deputy Head*. Not everyone reading this will want to follow Adam's path, but I share his story to illustrate what is possible. His willingness to continue developing professionally during his temporary work gave him the building blocks for an accomplished and inspiring career in education.

Learning to Teach in Other People's Classrooms – Adam Kohlbeck

I qualified as a teacher in July 2010. I had managed to get a place on a highly sought-after graduate teacher programme (GTP). At the time, it was one of the few paid routes you could take into teaching, and so the fact I had managed to get a place had given me confidence at the start of my training year. The year didn't go quite as I had hoped. My mentor was not the most interested of individuals and I flew somewhat under the radar. Looking back, I think there were some concerns about my progress; but by the time they surfaced, I was too close to the end of the programme for anyone to take the unpleasant step of having a difficult conversation with me about the lack of effectiveness of my actual teaching. So, I qualified, blissfully unaware of my lack of preparedness for what was to follow.

I had always been told, growing up, that I should be a teacher – 'You're so good with kids', 'they really look up to you'. It turns out that teaching them is an awful lot different to entertaining them at a family Christmas party and comes with a fair amount more accountability. My NQT year (as it was called then – now ECT), got off to an awful start. It was in fact so bad that at Christmas of my first term, the headteacher sat me down and said something along the lines of: 'Adam, we think you're a nice guy and we also think you haven't had the best training. We don't think you're a lost cause, but we also have Ofsted coming any day and frankly, we don't want them seeing you'. They offered to pay me for an additional six weeks, set me up with a good supply agency and waved goodbye to me at the end of that week. At the time, I thought it was terribly decent of them to show such compassion. Looking back through a slightly more cynical lens, six weeks' pay and the best supply agent I've ever worked with probably says more about how keen they were to see the back of me!

In hindsight, I can't blame them. I had an observation in a science lesson five weeks in, and in the feedback, my mentor said: 'You basically tried to teach them everything of a six-week unit in one lesson and you tried to do it by just talking at them nonstop for 45 minutes'. She continued, with clear sarcasm, 'I wondered if I had stayed longer if you were even going to give them an activity to do or if the whole lesson was going to be you talking at them!' She was joking, of course. I think my reaction concealed quite well than my plan had indeed been to talk at them for about another 15 minutes before drawing my sermon to a close and moving onto computing.

My final stand at the school was a trip to the National Gallery. I had visited the gallery in advance of the trip, planned out exactly where we would go, the explanations I would give for each of the paintings we would visit and the route we would take to maximise our time. I remember standing next to one particular painting, giving an in-depth analysis of the symbolism of the heavy velvet curtains in the picture and how these represented the weight of emotion that the protagonist felt weighing him down. As I delivered my explanation, I was aware of people walking past in increasing numbers which made me feel even more confident as the crowds I had been so concerned about seemed to be dispersing. We would soon have the gallery almost entirely to ourselves, I thought. A few moments later, I was approached by a member of museum staff who asked if we had been in Room 42. I proudly replied that we had and reeled off the works that we had been analysing while in that particular gallery. She asked me if I had a black Nike bag, and I replied that I did. I looked down to find that I didn't have it with me. I looked back up at her as she told me that I had left it in Room 42 and had triggered a complete evacuation of the entire gallery as they believed it be a bomb scare. As I dutifully conducted my head count in Trafalgar Square, I sensed the end was nigh.

So, having had such a rocky start, I was confronted with the reality that I wasn't ready for classroom teaching – yet. I decided that I would take a conscious positivity into my supply career and use it as my own self-directed training ground. For the next year and a half I completed four long-term supply assignments with the agency that the headteacher had almost forcibly signed me up to. I'll be forever grateful to that agency for the patience they gave me initially. I was going through a pretty horrendous personal relationship at the time that resulted in some nasty scars, both emotional and physical, and they were great supports to me while I navigated that particular turmoil. I bought myself a copy of *Teach Like a Champion* (Lemov, 2010), and each week I would study one technique over the weekend and then spend all week implementing and iterating, noting the different adaptations that were needed to it across different subjects, age groups and individuals. I repeated that every week for a year, and I slowly started to feel that I had some conscious control over my own practice. I knew why I was doing certain things in the way that I was doing them. I also recognised that these techniques weren't a silver bullet. Sometimes, they wouldn't work and I wasn't always sure why. Overall, though, I was getting better.

That sense of gradual improvement was knocked a bit each time I reached the end of a term and the school decided not to take me on permanently. Their explanations ranged from 'You just aren't strong enough for what the school needs in its current state' to 'We're really sorry, we just don't have any long-term vacancies' (they literally had a job advert in TES at the time). So, while I felt I was getting better – in fact, I *knew* I was getting better – it hadn't quite bled into my consistent practice yet. I think that's a really important thing for teachers to understand. It's a bit like going to the gym. I feel myself getting a bit stronger, a bit fitter all the time. I notice that I don't feel quite the same desperation for oxygen at the end of my 5k as I did four weeks ago. My wife says that I don't look any different, though. Then, maybe 8–12 weeks down the line, other people do start noticing a difference. Teaching is a bit like that. You feel you are getting better. It starts to feel different. Others might not see it, though, until further down the line. Don't let that convince you that are deluded – trust your gut.

I think that's the main challenge of supply – trusting and believing in yourself. A good chunk of supply teachers are there because something hasn't gone right in the schools they used to work in. That can mean that when another headteacher says 'I just don't quite see it', you convince yourself that the improvements you have been feeling were imaginary. That's not true. It just takes time for others to see the products of the improvements that you can feel because they are happening to you.

I'd love to say that my fourth long-term supply gig led to the happy ending of my getting back into the classroom with a full-time, permanent job. Sadly, that's not the case. They let me go, and as I was on the train home, I phoned a friend who asked if I had applied for the job at the school just down the road from my parents. I wasn't even aware of the job, but I had previously had a contract with the school to provide after-school tennis lessons (I ran a tennis coaching business between the ages of 16 and 22). My mum also worked at the school as a receptionist. Looking back, it says something about the belief my mum had in my teaching ability that she never even mentioned the vacancy to me! I had even completed my Year 10 work experience at the school. It was worth a shot, especially as I was convinced that I was finally improving and I felt ready to find a home again – somewhere where I could focus even more on developing my teaching without the pressure of having to win a permanent contract. I phoned the school, only to be told that the deadline had passed. I was disappointed but then, the headteacher phoned back and said that if I completed an application that night, they would still consider me. The long and short of it is that I got the interview and got the job.

While the road from then on has never been smooth, I feel I have never looked back. I also know that supply not only saved my career, but it also helped me thrive. Had it not been for those months of facing my own humility every day going into a school where I didn't really feel like a part of the team, I may not have had the single-minded commitment to my own improvement. All I cared about was getting a bit better at teaching every week, and supply gave me the space to do that. I wasn't in the staff room getting to know people because they didn't see me as worth their time because I was supply – but that gave me the space to focus on my teaching and my teaching only.

Now, in my leadership role, I try to make sure that anyone in our organisation on supply is part of the team from day one. We have three teachers who have come to us through supply agencies. One is a year group leader, another is the union rep and the third has been with us for only two weeks and is one of the main contributors in our weekly PD meetings. The point is that they are all part of the community. That's what we need to do as school leaders. We are part of an ecosystem consisting of multiple communities – our local community, our school community, the community of teachers and professionals. We need to induct people into these communities when they join us. When they join us from supply, we need to induct them, knowing that they probably feel more outside of these communities than anyone else. Of course, they need to read all the policies and the codes of conduct and sign up to the marking policy (if you still insist on getting teachers to do written marking), but they also need to be inducted into how the community works and supports each other.

Our latest recruit from a supply agency is part of our coaching programme and part of a teacher round table currently looking at how we teach history across the school. We are investing in them from the start, not because we want to be seen to be

> investing in everyone, but because we genuinely believe that teachers, all teachers, are worth investing in. Supply teaching taught me a lesson that has stayed with me forever, which is that if you take a teacher who, despite having had challenges and difficulties in one school, is still committed to the profession enough to keep coming back and stay determined to improve, and you put that teacher in an environment where they aren't judged but are given the conditions to develop, they'll probably be one of the most driven teachers in your team. Those of us who have had the knocks and have worked our way back up have a special quality to offer our school communities. The rest of us, if we want to benefit from that quality, have to make sure that supply teachers are as much a part of our community as anyone else.
>
> As I write this, I think back to yesterday. I spoke to our latest supply recruit in my office at the end of the day. At one point of the conversation, she said, 'Doing supply, I really get to see …' I asked her to rephrase, and she said, 'Doing supply, I really saw …' She's part of our community now, and we couldn't be more proud of the fact that she is.

I.3 The Goal of This Book

A recent Department for Education (DfE) survey highlights the varied routes into temporary teaching, with around half of temporary teachers having previously held permanent posts, including those approaching retirement, returning from maternity leave or in the early stages of their careers (DfE, 2023).

The most common reason for choosing temporary teaching is flexibility. Around half of respondents said that it gives them greater control over their time and workload. Interestingly, the main reasons people gave for leaving permanent posts were exactly that – workload and stress.

Perhaps more surprisingly, 44% of temporary teachers have never been in a permanent teaching role. Many come straight into it from training or move into it from roles such as cover supervisor or tutor.

For me, though, the most striking figures are those about retention. Almost 40% of temporary teachers say they would consider a permanent post if one were offered. Nearly half are thinking about leaving supply altogether, but crucially, around half of those say it's because they want to find a permanent role.

I went into teaching to make the biggest possible difference to the lives of young people. Like many educators both permanent and temporary, education gave me the chance of a better life, and I've always wanted to help others find the same opportunity. But right now, our profession is in crisis. Recruitment and retention are serious challenges, and many teachers are being driven away by high workload and stress.

The deeper purpose of this book is rooted in the same reason I first stepped into a classroom: To make a difference to students' lives. This time, though, my focus is on the students taught by temporary teachers – the young people whose learning depends on a workforce that is too often overlooked.

My hope is that this book helps temporary teachers feel genuinely empowered and confident in their roles – whether they plan to remain in temporary roles or eventually move into a permanent post. For those considering permanent work as their next step, I hope it provides the belief and practical support needed to take it.

For those who choose temporary teaching as a long-term path, this book is equally for you. Research on intrinsic motivation, particularly self-determination theory, suggests that fulfilment and sustained motivation are driven by three core psychological needs – competence, autonomy and relatedness (Deci & Ryan, 2000). For temporary teachers, the need for belonging is often the most difficult to meet, making the development of competence and autonomy especially important.

The purpose of this book is simple: to give temporary teachers the structures, strategies and confidence to bring autonomy and skill into every classroom they enter – adding value to lessons, supporting students effectively and finding fulfilment in the work they do.

References

Deci, E. L., & Ryan, R. M. (2000). Intrinsic and extrinsic motivations: Classic definitions and new directions. *Contemporary Educational Psychology*, 25(1), 54–67.

Department for Education (DfE) (2023). *School Workforce in England: November 2023.* London: Department for Education.

Lemov, D. (2010). *Teach like a Champion: 49 Techniques that Put Students on the Path to College.* San Francisco, CA: Jossey-Bass.

1 First-Day Fundamentals

1.1 Understanding the Realities of Temporary Teaching

Before exploring the practical realities of a temporary teacher's first day in school, it's worth grounding this chapter in lived experience. Much of what follows – the uncertainty, the rapid decision-making, the need for adaptable routines – is best understood not through theory alone, but through the experiences of those who have lived it.

This chapter opens with a case study from Alex Fairlamb, co-author of *The Scaffolding Effect*, a book focused on building classrooms with high expectations and strong instructional support. When I first approached Alex to contribute to this book, I asked her to write about how temporary teachers can provide effective scaffolding for students despite having limited planning time and little prior knowledge of pupils' needs. She agreed immediately – but what emerged was something even more valuable.

Like many educators featured in this book, Alex's journey into teaching began through temporary work. Her experience as a cover supervisor not only shaped her classroom practice but fundamentally altered her understanding of what it means to teach under pressure, without familiarity and with very little margin for error. Her story captures many of the realities temporary teachers face on their first days in school – uncertainty, behavioural challenges, shifting expectations – and offers a powerful lens through which to view the rest of this chapter.

Finding My Feet as a Cover Supervisor – Alex Fairlamb

When I decided to become a teacher, I applied for my PGCE and I was not successful in securing a place on the course. The feedback given to me was that for me to get onto such a competitive course, I needed to build up my experience working in schools. That year, I worked as a cover supervisor within a secondary school. I did not know it at the time that I was given the job, but this would be incredibly valuable experience which helped to prepare me for when I was successful in starting my teacher training year.

DOI: 10.4324/9781003780410-2

What Are the Challenges of Being a Supply/Cover Teacher?

- No two days are the same. The nature of supply/cover is that you are deployed to cover expected but also unexpected absences. That will mean that there is often no consistency in what subjects and classes you teach. This means that on a daily basis you are starting the day without a clear steer of what you can expect from the day, which can be unsettling.
- You can be deployed beyond your specialism. If you are a trained geography teacher or someone hoping to train as one, you could be teaching sports, art and more. This can be difficult because you may find explaining tasks more difficult and struggle to explain the content, or provide support for those who need scaffolding to access the information or to undertake the skill.
- Children like routine and typicality. Whilst some students may complain about their usual teacher, a change in their routine and a new person with unknown boundaries and limited knowledge of you creates an environment ripe for boundary pushing. Students may therefore challenge your behaviour management strategies (not listening when you ask for silence) and your knowledge of the behaviour systems within that school (for example, 'That's not the rule here', or 'My teacher usually let's me go to the toilet').
- Processing information and data quickly. This can include seating plans, task instructions, where resources are and information about key students (such as Educational Health Care Plans, toilet passes, behaviour reports, etc.). Added to that, there could also be a note about unusual changes to the school day due to things such as vaccinations and photographs which could be taking place during a lesson that you are covering.
- Layout of the school building. It can be challenging in some schools to work out where classrooms are, and this can impede your ability to transition quickly and smoothly from one classroom to another. Struggling to find a room or being given lessons on opposite ends of a building can impact on a smooth start to a lesson due to lateness.
- Cover not being set, the quality not being to standard or the children struggling to access what has been set. I have seen a full range of cover left from high-quality instructions and cover to Post-it note instructions, colouring in tasks and wordsearches. It is also possible that if a lesson requires using technology, the technology could fail to work. Having core strategies such as how to create flash cards, how to create mind maps and how to create other revision tools means that irrespective of the subject, if the students have access to books/knowledge organisers, you can quickly adapt the lesson to focus on consolidation. Whilst this might not be the plans left and could be frustrating to those who have left the cover, as someone who has experienced the work not landing and my subject knowledge not being there (maths with Year 11), this provides a more likely situation of them engaging in useful learning.

What Are the Benefits of Gaining Supply/Cover Teacher Experience?

- Developing confidence. As someone who had not stood up and delivered information to groups of children before, this exposed me to multiple opportunities to build up my confidence with walking into a large classroom and addressing 30 or so expectant faces.
- Developing resilience. As a supply teacher, behaviour can often be more challenging as students react to the lack of routine and push the boundaries of the expectations that a teacher may have. This can create a sense of worry about teaching certain classes or students. Being a supply/cover teacher creates opportunities for you to reflect upon and recover from tricky or difficult lessons, then rebuild to try again the next time.
- Developing behaviour management skills and building relationships. Linked to the previous point, you often have to respond to challenging behaviour, teach hard to reach children that you have very little contextual knowledge about and try to forge a relationship of trust and respect. My experiences as a cover supervisor enabled me to work out strategies and approaches that did and did not work. For example, trying to be less strict than their usual teacher by letting certain behaviour slip in order to curry favour did not work. Students realise that you have lowered your expectations of their conduct and will continue to test boundaries. However, using the names on the seating plan to address students personally when answering questions about the work or providing support helps to breakdown initial barriers.
- Developing your knowledge of other subjects. By teaching lessons beyond your specialism, you are exposed to multiple opportunities to see how lessons in other subject areas are taught. This helps you to identify connections between subjects, including your own, as well as being to see how knowledge and skills are developing in disciplinary ways elsewhere.

Why This Experience Matters

Alex's account captures something that many temporary teachers recognise immediately: the emotional and cognitive load of walking into an unfamiliar environment with limited information, limited preparation time and high expectations placed upon you.

Her experience highlights several of the realities that define temporary teaching:

- the absence of routine
- the pressure of managing behaviour without established relationships
- the need to adapt instantly to unfamiliar subjects and systems
- the challenge of maintaining confidence while still learning the role

These are not minor inconveniences. They are structural features of temporary teaching – and they shape how teachers think, act and form professional habits. This is where the idea of stasis becomes particularly important.

1.2 Stasis: A Double-Edged Sword for Temporary Teachers

Every temporary teacher knows the feeling of arriving at a new school with little idea of what awaits them. The uncertainty can be daunting – especially when 'the call' comes early in the morning, leaving just enough time to grab a coffee and figure out the route before the day begins.

Peps McCrea once argued that teaching is harder than brain surgery – and it's difficult to disagree. His reasoning is striking: brain surgeons operate on one patient who is unconscious, surrounded by expensive, precise equipment, with monitors providing real-time feedback and a team of specialists supporting them at every step (McCrea, 2023). Teachers, by contrast, work with around 30 students all very much awake, all at different stages of understanding, often with limited resources and equipment that has seen better days. If you're lucky, there's a teaching assistant in the room – though sometimes there really should be three.

For temporary teachers, all of these factors apply, but with an added layer of difficulty: you've never met the students before. The work left behind might not engage them for a full hour, and you're often unaware of the school's routines, expectations or behaviour systems. The result is a job that can, at times, feel nearly impossible.

Most experienced temporary teachers eventually develop their own routines and coping strategies for these situations. Still, this chapter feels essential, not only for new temporary teachers, who often ask, 'What should I expect when I arrive at a new school?', but also for seasoned professionals. Even the most experienced teachers can fall into *teacher stasis*.

The dictionary defines *stasis* as 'a state of static balance or equilibrium'. In this context, stasis refers to the way our professional habits become fixed – stable, comfortable and resistant to change. For temporary teachers, who operate in unpredictable environments, recognising and challenging this stasis is key to continued growth and adaptability.

Stasis, in teaching, is both a comfort and a constraint. It gives us the security of knowing what to do, but it can quietly stop us from growing.

Every temporary teacher develops routines that bring stability – how lessons begin, how behaviour is managed, how feedback is given. These routines are essential. They free up mental space so we can focus on what really matters: our students. Without them, every lesson would feel like starting from scratch. Stasis allows us to function in a demanding environment. It's the reason we can handle 30 different learners at once, remember where we were in the lesson sequence and respond calmly when something goes wrong.

For temporary teachers, that stability is even more valuable. Walking into an unfamiliar school each day, you need your own personal anchor points – habits and systems you can rely on when everything else is new. Your go-to strategies for starting a lesson, building rapport or regaining attention are what make the job possible. In this sense, stasis is your ally; it's the foundation that allows you to stay composed amid uncertainty.

But there's a risk hidden in that same strength. Once our habits become automatic, they're hard to question. We stop noticing them. A routine that once helped us stay afloat can, over time, become a barrier to improvement. This is the tension at the heart of teaching: we need stability to survive, but change to grow.

For a permanent teacher, stasis might mean settling into patterns that worked five years ago but no longer match the needs of a new cohort. For a temporary teacher, it might mean relying on the same approach in every school – even when the behaviour systems, expectations and culture are completely different. The habits that once made you efficient can start to make you inflexible.

True professional growth comes from noticing when your routines are helping and when they're holding you back. That requires conscious reflection – a willingness to pause and ask: *Is this strategy effective here? Or am I doing it because it's comfortable?*

The goal isn't to abandon stasis. It's to use it wisely. Stability gives you the bandwidth to adapt; adaptation keeps that stability relevant. In practice, that might mean changing just one small element – how you start a lesson, how you give instructions, how you frame expectations – and then allowing that new behaviour to settle before taking on another. Sustainable change happens when we build new routines on top of stable foundations.

For temporary teachers, mastering this balance is key. You need to carry enough stability with you to handle any classroom, but enough flexibility to fit into a new environment each day. The best temporary teachers aren't just adaptable – they know when to rely on habit and when to reinvent it.

So, the rest of this chapter will focus on those *first-day fundamentals* – the hinge points in a temporary teacher's day that you know will come. The goal is to highlight them, to help you reflect on your routines and to question whether they still work for you. What tweaks could you make to improve the experience – not just for your students, but for yourself?

These hinge points – arriving at reception, meeting the cover supervisor, setting the tone as you enter the classroom, starting the lesson, managing behaviour and closing the session – are the moments that can make or break the day. By preparing for them deliberately, you can reduce uncertainty, strengthen your sense of control and transform what might feel like chaos into calm, purposeful teaching.

1.3 Getting the Basics Right: Preparation, Arrival and Professionalism

For temporary teachers, preparation begins long before you walk through the school gates. The difference between a calm start and a stressful day often lies in what you've done *before you even leave home.*

Before You Leave Home

Start with the essentials. For UK educators, ensure your DBS is on the Update Service so schools can verify it instantly – this saves time and avoids unnecessary admin. Keep your own 'supply kit' ready: pens, a USB stick, basic stationery and a few reliable lesson activities you can adapt to any class. Many teachers recommend short, ten-minute tasks for cover lessons or subjects outside your specialism, such as quick discussion prompts, literacy warm-ups or simple drama games.

It's also worth thinking about your professional security. Join a union; they provide invaluable advice and protection if things don't go as planned. When working through agencies, agree upfront on cancellation terms; you should still be paid if a booking is cancelled at short notice. Fees are negotiable, particularly if you're taking on responsibilities beyond the lesson itself, like parents' evenings or report writing. Some temporary teachers also register with multiple agencies to keep their options open – you're not obliged to tell them who else you work for.

Temporary teachers should also leverage networks, for example Facebook groups like the network of supply teachers. These communities offer professional development, advice and connections that can make the work less isolating, especially for those moving from school to school.

Food and drink are critical. Bring your own lunch or snacks – it's rare for temporary teachers to have guaranteed access to a canteen, and queues or limited options can eat into your break. A reusable water bottle and a flask of tea or coffee help you stay comfortable and focused throughout the day. Don't forget practical clothing considerations too: comfortable shoes and layers are important in classrooms with unpredictable temperatures.

Finally, plan your transport. Know the route, travel time and parking options, and keep any necessary car park fobs or access passes ready. These small practical details reduce stress before you even arrive.

When You Arrive

The first few minutes in a new school set the tone for the day. Access to clear information can transform that experience. A seating plan, even a rough one, helps you connect names and faces quickly. Two copies of a register – one to mark, one to make notes – allow you to track attendance and behaviour efficiently. Always ask for a copy of the behaviour policy; knowing how the school expects you to respond to issues helps you remain consistent and confident.

Equally important is knowing who to contact in case of a safeguarding concern. Ask for the names and locations of the designated safeguarding leads (DSLs) and any other key safeguarding staff. Being clear on this from the start ensures you can act quickly and appropriately if any issues arise.

Take a few moments to understand the school's routines. Find out the procedures for fire drills, where first aid points are and how lunch arrangements work. Knowing these basic systems helps you feel confident and reduces unnecessary stress during the day.

If time allows, introduce yourself to a neighbouring teacher or the department lead. They can often tell you which students are particularly helpful or may need extra support. A quick conversation like this can save frustration later. Ask about lesson timings and bell schedules too – these vary from school to school, and knowing them helps you manage transitions smoothly.

Make sure you know how to access essential equipment and technology: computers, projectors, interactive whiteboards or any online platforms the school uses. Familiarity with these tools prevents unnecessary delays and allows you to focus on teaching rather than troubleshooting technical issues.

When it comes to marking, keep expectations realistic. Unless you've agreed otherwise, live marking, self-assessment or peer feedback during the lesson is sufficient. Your role is to ensure learning continues smoothly, not to take on the full-time teacher's marking load.

Settling In

If the staffroom feels unwelcoming, don't take it personally – use your break to get admin done or prep for the next lesson instead.

The consistent message from experienced temporary teachers is simple: preparation and attention to practical details can transform a day from stressful to manageable. When these basics are in place, temporary teachers can focus on what really matters – connecting with students, delivering lessons with confidence and leaving a positive impression wherever they go.

Before You Leave

The end of a placement is just as important as the start. Taking a few moments to leave a professional impression can make a big difference, especially if you hope to return to the school in the future.

Leave brief notes for the class teacher or relevant staff. Keep them concise – highlight key achievements, student contributions or anything that needs follow-up. Avoid overloading them with details they may not have time to read. A short, clear note can help maintain continuity for the next lesson and shows your professionalism.

If you have the opportunity, say goodbye to any senior staff you interacted with. If you enjoyed your time at the school, don't be afraid to express it. Mention specific things you appreciated about the school, and name a few students who worked particularly hard or made a positive impression. These small gestures leave a lasting impression and demonstrate your engagement and care.

1.4 A Checklist for Confidence and Consistency

Before You Leave Home

- Pack essentials: ID, DBS certificate, pen, notepad and any agency paperwork.
- Bring your own lunch, snacks and a bottle of water – it's not always easy to buy food in school.
- Prepare a few adaptable lesson activities or short games in case the set work isn't engaging or appropriate.
- Dress professionally but comfortably – you never know what subject or room you'll be teaching in.
- Check your route and travel time; aim to arrive early enough to familiarise yourself with the site.

When You Arrive

- Ask for two copies of the register – one to mark, one for notes.
- Request a seating plan or class list, even if incomplete.
- Get a copy of the behaviour policy and clarify any reward or sanction systems.
- Identify safeguarding contacts – the DSL and deputies – and where they can be found.
- Find out key school routines: fire drill procedure, first aid points and lunch arrangements.
- Ask about lesson timings, bells and transition cues.
- Introduce yourself to a nearby teacher or department lead – they often know useful context about classes or students.
- Check access to equipment and technology: computers, projectors, interactive whiteboards or online platforms.
- Locate staff facilities: staffroom, toilets and where you can safely store your belongings.

During the Day

- Use live marking, self-assessment or peer marking – avoid extensive written marking unless it is pre-agreed.
- Note any safeguarding, behaviour or attendance concerns promptly.
- Take your lunch break; use the time to reset.

Before You Leave

- Leave a short note for the class teacher summarising what was covered and any follow-up needed.
- Mention any students who worked particularly well or need extra support.
- Say goodbye to key staff or the person who booked you – a friendly, professional sign-off goes a long way.
- If you enjoyed the school, let them know – a quick thank-you or positive comment about the students or environment can leave a lasting impression.
- Double-check whether you've signed out and collected any personal belongings.

1.5 Reflective Prompts for Temporary Teachers

One of the challenges with temporary teaching is the lack of structured professional development. Yes, you can read, watch videos or sometimes chat with other temporary teachers, but there's often no one systematically looking after your professional development. In permanent teaching roles, it's common practice to receive regular feedback on your lessons – a practice that can help combat the effects of stasis.

Without that support, it becomes even more vital for temporary teachers to give themselves time to reflect. Taking a few moments after each placement to consider what went well and what could be improved helps you grow as a professional and build routines that truly work for you. Here are some questions you may consider at the end of a placement:

- *Preparation check*: Did I pack everything I needed before leaving home? What could I add or improve for next time?
- *Arrival routine*: How quickly was I able to locate key information (register, seating plan, behaviour policy, safeguarding contacts)? Did I feel confident in the first few minutes of class?
- *Routines and systems*: Was I clear on fire drills, first aid and lunch routines? Did any uncertainty cause unnecessary stress?
- *Lesson management*: Were my emergency or adaptable activities effective? Which worked well, and which could be improved?
- *Technology and equipment*: Did I have the access I needed to teach effectively? How could I prepare better for different setups next time?
- *Professional comfort*: Did I have access to staff facilities (kitchen, toilet, workspace)? How did this affect my focus and wellbeing?
- *Professional courtesy*: Did I leave clear notes and communicate positively with staff before leaving? What might I do differently to make a stronger impression next time?

- *Networking and support*: Have I connected with other supply teachers, networks or unions? Could I use these connections more effectively?
- *Reflection on flexibility*: Which routines worked well across different schools? Which needed adjusting, and how might I adapt them next time?

Every temporary teacher knows that the first day can feel overwhelming, but it's also an opportunity. The preparation, organisation and reflection you invest now don't just make your day easier – they allow you to teach with confidence and clarity, whatever the classroom throws at you.

Having established these practical foundations, the next chapter moves into developing the teaching techniques that turn competence into excellence. With the groundwork laid, you're ready to focus on the craft of teaching and how to make every lesson count.

Reference

McCrea, P. (2023). *Developing Expert Teaching: A Practical Guide to Designing Effective Professional Development, for Others and Ourselves*. Independently published.

2 Classroom Strategies for Temporary Teachers

2.1 The Role of the Temporary Teacher: What You Can and Cannot Control

As a temporary teacher on a short-term placement, perhaps lasting up to a couple of weeks, it is likely you will be expected to follow a lesson plan. If the absence was planned, this plan may have been written by the teacher you are covering. However, for last-minute absences, it is often provided by one of their superiors.

Unfortunately, in some cases, the work you are given may not be adequate to fill an entire lesson. This can be frustrating and may make you feel as though you are not trusted with quality work. There are many reasons this can happen. The absent teacher may be ill and unable to prepare a lesson for you to the quality they would have wanted, or the colleague tasked with providing last-minute work may have their own responsibilities to manage. The point is that while it is easy for temporary teachers to take this personally, the inadequacy of the lesson plan usually has nothing to do with you.

One principle I try to live by as a temporary teacher comes from Stephen Covey's *The 7 Habits of Highly Effective People*. Covey emphasizes being proactive, reminding us that 'between stimulus and response there is a space (Covey, 1989). In that space is our power to choose our response. In our response lies our growth and our freedom' (p. 69). This idea is illustrated in a story he shares about a father on the subway with his unruly children. Other passengers are frustrated, but when someone asks the father to control them, he responds, 'Sorry, their mother has just died. I am not sure what to do'. Suddenly, everyone's frustration turns to empathy.

It is easy to feel frustrated when you enter a classroom and the work provided is not sufficient, but it is important to remember that this is out of your control. You have no way of knowing all the factors that led to the situation. When this happens, I remind myself of Covey's story and words. They help me approach the class with patience and understanding rather than frustration.

DOI: 10.4324/9781003780410-3

This chapter is dedicated to what is in your control. How can you develop your toolkit to improve the lesson to support student learning?

Let's begin with a definition of learning. While the concept has been widely debated in education, and there are many interpretations, I will use the one provided by the National Research Council (2000), a respected U.S. body that offers research-based guidance on science and education. According to the Council, learning is a process resulting from experience that leads to a change in knowledge, skills, attitudes, or behaviours, which may be temporary or permanent.

Let's break this down in terms of a priority for temporary teachers, First, let's look at the things you could attempt to change – knowledge, skills, attitudes and behaviours. I want to split them into two groups:

1. Knowledge and skills
2. Attitudes and behaviours

It is possible for a temporary teacher to influence a student's behaviour, but any change is likely to be short-lived. For example, a student might talk over you while you are explaining a task, and something you do causes them to stop. The strategy may work in that moment, and perhaps for the rest of the lesson, but the child is unlikely to behave the same way for a different teacher in a different lesson. Even if you give a ten-minute, Oscar-worthy inspirational speech about the importance of good behaviour, its long-term impact will probably be minimal. In the next chapter I discuss strategies that temporary teachers can use to improve behaviour and attitudes, even if only for a limited period.

For now, let's focus on knowledge and skills. The work we are given as temporary teachers is likely to produce only a short-term change in knowledge, regardless of what we do. A student may leave the lesson knowing something they did not know when they walked in, but there is a good chance they will forget it by tomorrow, and almost a certainty that it will be forgotten by the following week. For us as temporary teachers, to have high expectations of our impact, we must aim to create a permanent change in a student's knowledge and skills. This is a challenging goal, but it is one we should set for ourselves, as it helps us feel that we have contributed meaningfully to the child's education, no matter how brief our time with them.

Before exploring the various techniques, we can use to increase the likelihood of permanent change, let's take a closer look at how learning happens. Some educators reading this book may already have formal training in areas such as working and long-term memory, cognitive load, the role of schemas, retrieval practice, metacognition, and dual coding. Each principle in this chapter is presented in two sections: first, the theory, and second, the application of that theory. You may choose to skip the theory for some or all of the principles, or simply skim it. What matters most in this chapter is understanding how to apply these ideas to support a permanent change in students' knowledge.

2.2 Working and Long-Term Memory

Working memory is the cognitive system responsible for temporarily holding and manipulating information. It has a limited capacity and duration, making it critical for processing new knowledge.

Long-term memory is the system where knowledge, skills and experiences are stored more permanently. Information is encoded from working memory into long-term memory, allowing it to be retained and retrieved over time.

The two systems are closely linked: working memory acts as a gateway, processing and organizing information before it is consolidated into long-term memory. Effective learning depends on the smooth interaction between these systems, as working memory manages immediate cognitive demands while long-term memory stores knowledge for future use.

Murdoch's (1962) free recall experiment provided key evidence for the existence of two distinct memory systems. Participants were asked to remember lists of words, and their recall showed two patterns. The primacy effect meant they remembered words from the beginning of the list more accurately. This is because when first hearing the list, participants had more time and mental space to rehearse and practise those early words, which increased the chance of the words being encoded into long-term memory. The recency effect meant they also remembered words from the end of the list more easily, since these were still active in working memory. However, Murdoch showed that the recency effect disappeared if participants completed a distracting task before recall, because working memory is fragile and easily disrupted. In contrast, the primacy effect remained, as those early items had already been stored more securely in long-term memory.

Building on this foundation, Craik and Tulving's (1975) levels of processing experiment demonstrated that it is not simply whether something is rehearsed that determines retention, but how deeply it is processed. In their study, participants were asked to carry out different kinds of tasks with words. At the shallowest level, they might judge whether a word was written in capital letters. At a slightly deeper level, they might decide whether it rhymed with another word. At the deepest level, they had to place the word into a meaningful sentence.

To put this into context, imagine students are given the word *river.*

- *Shallow processing*: They are asked, *'Is the word written in capital letters?'* (Yes/No).
- *Intermediate processing*: They are asked, *'Does the word rhyme with "giver"?'* (Yes/No).
- *Deep processing*: They are asked, *'Would the word fit in the sentence "The ____ flows through the valley"?'* (Yes/No).

The results showed that words that required deep, semantic processing—thinking about their meaning and relationship to other ideas—were remembered far better than those processed only at a superficial level. The implication is clear for teaching: if we want students to retain knowledge, we must design tasks and questions that push them beyond surface features and encourage them to think hard about meaning, connections and application. Simply exposing students to information, or asking them to notice shallow details, is unlikely to result in permanent learning.

This brings me to one of the most widely cited ideas in educational psychology. As Daniel Willingham (2009, p. 47) argues, 'memory is the residue of thought'. If we want students to remember something, we must first ensure that they are thinking deeply about it.

Application of Theory

It is possible that lesson plans left for temporary teachers will include some form of rehearsal. The lesson may involve introducing new knowledge through a video, a text for students to read or a PowerPoint for you to guide them through. In other cases, there may be no new knowledge at all, and instead the focus will be on revisiting what students have already been taught by their regular teacher. In both situations, the common-thread next step is rehearsal; students are asked to practise either newly introduced material or knowledge they have previously encountered.

It is far less common for temporary teachers to be left work that encourages students to think deeply about what they are learning. This, however, is where the temporary teacher's skillset comes into play. The real question is: What techniques can we bring into a lesson at short notice to increase the chances that students will actually remember what they have learned? We may never be in the room long enough to see the impact of these choices, but we can leave at the end of the day knowing we did our utmost to give students the best chance of making their learning stick.

'I Used to Think … Now I Think …'

One simple technique you can use, even with no preparation, is to ask students to complete the sentence: 'I used to think … Now I think …'

For example, in a science lesson on forces, you might say:

> Before today's lesson, you might have thought that heavier objects fall faster than lighter ones. Now, after watching the video and doing the activity, how would you complete this sentence: I used to think … Now I think …?

A student might respond:

> I used to think heavy things fall faster, but now I think all objects fall at the same speed unless air resistance slows them down.

This short reflection encourages students to process the meaning of the knowledge more deeply, strengthening the chances it will be remembered

Word, Phrase, Sentence

Another task that works well is to ask students to focus on the language of a text or video by choosing:

- A *word* that captured their attention or struck them as powerful.
- A *phrase* that moved, engaged, or provoked them.
- A *sentence* that felt meaningful or captured the core idea of the text.

For example, in an English lesson using Martin Luther King Jr.'s 'I Have a Dream' speech, one student might select the word 'freedom', another the phrase 'fierce urgency of now', and another the sentence 'I have a dream that one day my children will not be judged by the color of their skin but by the content of their character'. The discussion that follows might highlight themes of justice, urgency, and equality. Students could then reflect that while these choices capture the speech's moral force, the theme of hope also needs to be considered.

This activity pushes students beyond surface recall and gets them thinking hard about meaning, structure and significance.

Magenta Principles

Another powerful approach that temporary teachers can draw on is Mike Hughes's Magenta Principles, which emphasise purposeful action, challenge and thinking over comfort (Hughes, 2013). Rather than passively receiving information, students should be prompted to sort key terms into groups, change ideas by rewriting or representing them differently, connect new knowledge to prior learning or real-life contexts, compare concepts to highlight similarities and differences, prioritise what is most important and explain their reasoning. These flexible, subject-neutral strategies can be used in any lesson, from science to English or maths, and are ideal for temporary teachers who want to deepen students' thinking without requiring extensive preparation.

Examples

- *Sort*: Give students key terms from the lesson – for example, in science, 'chlorophyll, sunlight, glucose, oxygen' – and ask them to group them in ways that make sense.
- *Change*: Ask students to rewrite a concept in their own words, such as summarising a paragraph from a text or explaining a maths rule to a younger student.
- *Connect*: Prompt students to link new knowledge to something familiar; e.g., 'How does this historical event affect life today?'
- *Compare*: Ask students to identify similarities and differences, like comparing two characters in a story or two methods for solving a maths problem.

- *Prioritise*: Have students decide what is most important from a short text or diagram.
- *Explain*: Get students to justify a choice or prediction, or answer briefly in a sentence.

Throughout this chapter, case studies from practising educators are used to illustrate how key strategies can be applied in real classroom contexts. These examples are intended to move beyond theory and show how effective practice looks in action, because the way a strategy is implemented is often just as important as the strategy itself. Thoughtful implementation increases clarity, consistency, and ultimately the likelihood of meaningful student engagement.

The first example comes from Ms Samayoa, a teacher based in California. As you read this case study, pay close attention to the level of structure, clarity and routine she establishes in her classroom. Consider how this compares to a more ad-hoc approach, such as simply writing on the board, 'If you've finished, compare the two characters'. Reflect on how the precision of Ms Samayoa's instructions shapes pupil behaviour, focus and learning, and how small differences in approach can have a significant impact on student engagement.

Structured Thinking Through Turn and Talk – Ms Samayoa

When students walk into their classroom and see a substitute teacher sitting at their teacher's desk, I wouldn't be surprised if their first thought is, 'Yes! Free time!'

For a substitute teacher, it can be difficult to set a serious tone in the classroom. There are 35 students who are unfamiliar with them, and they are sitting in a classroom that is only temporarily theirs. But this can be mediated by providing structure in the classroom through explicit instruction.

For example, let's go over how a substitute teacher might implement turn and talk in the classroom. If you are not familiar with turn and talk, it is a strategy for class participation. It's how I get every student thinking and talking without losing the room. As a substitute, I can't assume students know my routines, so I provide structure by making my turn and talk instructions explicit.

This is how it would take place:

1. *Start with an introduction.*
   'Hello everyone. My name is Ms. Samayoa and I will be your substitute teacher today. I see that we are going over ionic and covalent compounds. We will review this content using turn and talks. Before we do any turn and talks, I'm going to teach you exactly how we do it in this room'.
2. *Assign partners.*
   'I see that you are in pairs. Student closest to the door, raise your hand'.
   I wait. I don't move on until every student that is closest to the door raises their hand.

'Good. You are Partner A. Hands down. Student farthest from the door, raise your hand'.

I wait. I don't move on until every student that is farthest from the door raises their hand.

'Good. You are Partner B. Hands down. Let's try that again so it's automatic. Partner A, raise your hand'.

Hands go up faster this time.

'Partner B, raise your hand'.

Hands go up faster this time too.

'Great! Let's get started!'

3. *Turn and talk structure*

'Here's how this works. Step one: I ask a question'. I pause.

'Step two: I give you thinking time. During thinking time, you do not answer out loud. This is silent thinking'.

I model what that looks like by standing still, eyes up, hand on the desk.

'Step three: you write your answer on paper silently. Pencil moving. When you're finished, pencils down'.

I mime writing, then deliberately place my pencil flat on the desk.

'Step four: Partner A shares with Partner B. Let me show you what listening looks like'.

I turn my body toward an imaginary partner. 'Eyes on the speaker. Mouth closed. No interrupting'.

Then I model responding. 'When it's your turn to respond, you might start with "I agree because …", "I want to add …" or "I thought something similar, but …"'.

4. *Practice*

'I am going to ask you a question. Remember to not say the answer out loud. Okay. Here it goes. "How does an ionic bond compare to a covalent bond?"' I provide wait time.

'Now everyone put your pencils up!' Pencils are up.

'Write down the answer to the question on your paper. When you are done, put your pencils down that way I know who is done and who is not'.

I wait until most pencils are flat. 'Partner A, share with Partner B'.

I circulate, reinforcing. 'Nice eye contact'. 'Good follow-up question'. 'That's what listening looks like'.

Then I reset them. 'Eyes on me in 3 … we are quieting down … 2 … everyone is facing forward … 1. Awesome'.

Giving students procedures on how to do certain tasks gives them the structure they need to complete them successfully. Structure also gives the substitute teacher credibility. It gives the impression that the substitute teacher knows what they are doing and is not intimidated by having unfamiliar students or by being in an unfamiliar classroom.

Getting the Most from Video and Text

If a video or text is long or challenging, consider breaking it in half. Pause midway and ask students to predict what will happen next – this keeps them thinking, engaged and active.

If the material is short and you anticipate extra time, show it multiple times. The first viewing is just to watch, the second to note key information and the third to write any questions they might have for their regular teacher.

2.3 Cognitive Load Theory

Cognitive load theory (CLT) explains how the brain processes information and why learning can be disrupted when demands exceed our cognitive capacity. Working memory has a limited capacity, so if too much information is presented at once, it becomes difficult to process, understand and store in long-term memory.

George Miller's famous 1956 experiment provides key evidence for this limitation. Miller asked participants to remember sequences of simple items, such as numbers, letters, or words. He discovered that people could reliably recall only about *7 ± 2 items* in a short-term memory task. For example, most people could remember a sequence of five to nine random digits, but sequences longer than this quickly exceeded their memory capacity. Miller (1956) referred to these 'chunks' of information as units of memory that the brain can handle at one time, highlighting the natural limit of working memory.

This 'magic number' demonstrates why overwhelming students with too many pieces of information at once can reduce learning: there simply isn't enough mental space to process everything effectively. It also explains why breaking complex information into smaller, meaningful chunks—or 'chunking'—can help learners manage cognitive load and increase the likelihood of encoding information into long-term memory.

CLT distinguishes between three types of cognitive load:

- *Intrinsic load*: The inherent difficulty of the material itself, which depends on the complexity of the content and the learner's prior knowledge.
- *Extraneous load*: Unnecessary cognitive effort imposed by poorly designed materials or instructions, such as confusing diagrams, irrelevant text or multitasking.
- *Germane load*: The cognitive effort devoted to processing, understanding and creating meaningful connections – exactly what supports learning and long-term memory formation.

For example, consider a student learning the water cycle for the first time. If a diagram is cluttered with extra labels and complicated arrows (high extraneous load), the student struggles to understand even the basic steps (intrinsic load). But if the diagram is clear, is simple and focuses attention on key processes, the student can devote mental effort to making connections and integrating the knowledge into long-term memory (germane load).

The implication is that effective teaching should manage cognitive load carefully. Material should be structured to reduce unnecessary distractions (extraneous load), match the learner's current knowledge (manageable intrinsic load) and encourage active processing and connections (germane load). Just as deep processing improves memory retention, reducing unnecessary cognitive burden allows working memory to focus on meaningful thinking, increasing the likelihood of permanent learning.

Application of Theory

Intrinsic Load

Let's break down how temporary teachers can apply this knowledge using the three types of cognitive load. First, intrinsic load refers to the inherent complexity of the material. Interestingly, when covering lessons as a temporary teacher, intrinsic load is often not the main issue. In fact, the opposite is more common: The work left for temporary cover is often too easy, as the regular teacher may be cautious about providing content that is too challenging. This is why temporary teachers benefit from having ready-made techniques to increase thinking and engagement during the lesson, as already discussed.

However, if you encounter material that is genuinely challenging – for example, if students have had several cover lessons in a row and are falling behind – there are several strategies you can use to manage intrinsic load while still promoting learning.

Identify Challenging Words

I once found myself teaching the same text across five consecutive lessons, each with a different age group ranging from 11 to 16. The challenge was immediately apparent: The text had not been adapted for the varying levels of cognitive development, reading fluency or prior knowledge of the students in front of me. What was appropriate for one class risked overwhelming another.

I was acutely aware that this mismatch would significantly increase cognitive load, particularly for younger students or those with limited background knowledge, who would be confronted with a high volume of unfamiliar vocabulary. Faced with this challenge, I needed a way to make the material more accessible without diluting its academic value. One effective solution was the deliberate pre-teaching of key vocabulary, allowing students to engage with the text more confidently and with reduced cognitive strain.

Preteaching Vocabulary to Reduce Cognitive Load – Jake Cowley

Supply teaching often means walking into a room mid-story: Unfamiliar pupils, unfamiliar texts, and vocabulary that students are expected to 'just get'. Tier 2 words are usually where things wobble. They're common in academic texts, rare in everyday speech and often waved through with a definition and a hope. Hope, as ever, is not a strategy.

Recent thinking from Carl Hendrick, alongside the older but sharper work of Siegfried Engelmann and Douglas Carnine, points to a blunt truth: When students misunderstand vocabulary, it's usually because the instruction was structurally unclear. Learners don't misgeneralise by accident; they misgeneralise because our examples allowed them to.

Pre-teaching Tier 2 words well is therefore less about charisma and more about design.

The first move is identifying the core meaning of the word – what Engelmann would call the 'sameness'. Before you teach, you must know what always stays true when the word is used correctly. For instinctively, that sameness is simple: an action that is immediate, is automatic and happens without conscious thought. Everything else – who is acting, where they are, whether it's a person or an animal – is irrelevant variation and must be deliberately changed across examples so students don't mistake context for meaning.

Once the sameness is clear, you translate it into a student-friendly definition that sits below their lexical bar. Not a dictionary definition, but one built from known words – to do something without thinking because it feels automatic. Break this into its critical attributes and make them visible. Many teachers pair each attribute with a consistent gesture, drawing on embodied cognition to signal meaning before language fully lands. This move is subtle, but powerful.

Next comes establishing the positive boundary. You present several examples that all share the critical attributes but vary widely in surface detail. A hand jerking away from a hot cup. A dog running to its owner during a storm. Arms flailing to regain balance on wet tiles. Your teacher phrasing stays constant, 'She did that instinctively', while the context shifts. Constancy in language highlights constancy in meaning.

Crucially, examples don't need to contain the target word. They need to show it. This prevents circular learning and forces conceptual understanding rather than parroting.

After that, you establish the negative boundary using minimal difference. You take one of your positive examples and alter only the critical feature. The child thinks about what to say, then acts. The chess player plans for ten minutes. The context stays similar; the thinking changes. Juxtaposing example and non-example back-to-back makes the boundary unmistakable. The word flips the moment conscious thought appears.

Only then do you check for generalisation. New examples. No labels. Students decide: 'Is this instinctively or not?' If they can reliably justify their answers, your instruction worked. If they can also explain why by using a sentence frame ('This is instinctively because …'), the word is moving from recognition to usable vocabulary.

Finally, you return to the text. Now the word instinctively in Matilda isn't decorative; it's anchored. Mrs Phelps didn't deliberate. Her body moved first. The rule applies.

> This approach, influenced by *Bringing Words to Life* (Beck et al., 2013) and *The Extended Mind in Action* (Wilson & Clark, 2009), replaces 'tell and hope' with deliberate design. For supply teachers especially, it offers something rare – a method that works even when relationships, routines and time are thin. When sameness and difference are carefully controlled, meaning sticks – not by luck, but by structure.

'I Say, You Say'

Another effective strategy when text can be challenging is to introduce 'I Say, You Say'. When reading a text aloud to the class, pause whenever you come across a key word or phrase. Say it clearly to the class, then have students repeat it back. This draws attention to essential concepts and keeps students actively engaged.

For example, if reading a science text about photosynthesis, you might pause at the phrase 'chlorophyll absorbs light energy' and say, 'Chlorophyll absorbs light energy!' The students then repeat, 'Chlorophyll absorbs light energy!' This reinforces understanding of a critical concept rather than just a single word, helping students to process and retain more complex ideas.

Choral Response

When I was a full-time teacher with my own classes, many of the strategies I used successfully depended on time, consistency and well-established routines. One such example was the use of mini-whiteboards. While handing out whiteboards may seem straightforward, using them effectively requires careful planning and strong classroom systems. Questions quickly arise: *What if students copy from one another? What if they write the wrong answer? What if the pens don't work?* For a temporary teacher stepping into an unfamiliar classroom, these variables can make an otherwise useful strategy difficult to manage.

A more accessible alternative, particularly in cover lessons is *choral response*. While it may not provide the same level of individual diagnostic insight as written responses, it is far easier to implement effectively in a short space of time. Choral response involves posing a question to the class and having all students respond aloud together, creating a shared moment of participation and focus.

As with the previous case studies, it is worth considering not just *what* the strategy is, but *how* it is implemented. When used well, choral response helps reduce cognitive load by directing students' attention to the most important information. At the same time, it sends a clear message about expectations: That learning is purposeful, participation is expected, and the temporary teacher is in control of the classroom environment. This combination of clarity and structure is particularly powerful in unfamiliar settings, where routines and relationships have yet to be established.

Setting the Tone: Using Choral Response to Establish Classroom Culture – Zach Groshell

For me, choral response is about tone-setting. When I would substitute teach, it was in schools serving disadvantaged populations. Subs often avoid these classrooms because of the reputation for poor behaviour. Tone and credibility are everything here. I have to show them, right from the start, that today will be productive.

I start at the threshold. I stand at the door, shake each student's hand, and ask their name. There's always a multi-part direction: Sit in your assigned seat. Pencil out. Ready to learn. Kids know, the moment they cross the line into the room, we're in a different kind of space. We don't mill around or wait for the clock. We begin.

Right away, I introduce choral response. 'Let me take a moment to teach you how to be my students. When I ask a question, you all answer – together'. I model it first, then we practice with easy questions:

'My name is Dr. Groshell. What is my name?' – 'Dr. Groshell!'

'What day is it?' – 'Monday!'

'What's two plus two?' – 'Four!'

I add positive narration to keep the energy up: 'That's what I'm talking about'. Or, 'Okay, okay, Ms. So-and-So didn't tell me you were this sharp'.

To embed choral response, I use the Teacher–Student Game. I draw a T-chart on the board: Teacher on one side, students on the other. The rules are simple – when the class responds together, they earn a point; when they don't, I do. Suddenly, students are leaning forward, eyes are tracking, voices are crisp. I set them up to win with the easy questions, which gives them an instant winning streak and momentum. The scoreboard becomes a visual reminder of the excellent behaviour they've somehow slipped into exhibiting.

By the time we move into the lesson, the tone has been set: This is serious, this is purposeful, this is learning. We choral read directions. We choral pronounce key words.

'Which problems are you going to do?' – '1 through 4!'

That's right. A point for you. Pencils moving. No time to waste.

There are several reasons for asking questions immediately after sharing information:

1. It keeps students alert, knowing that they may be called on at any moment.
2. It reduces intrinsic load, by breaking down the task and increasing the number of pupils who can respond successfully.
3. The collective response allows you to quickly identify misunderstandings and challenge students who later claim the material was too difficult.

Extraneous Load

This can be particularly challenging as a temporary teacher. If the lesson materials are poorly designed, it may feel difficult – but it is not impossible – to adapt on the fly.

First, if a teacher provides multiple instructions at once, consider sharing only one instruction at a time. For example, a lesson might ask students to:

- Read a poem
- Identify metaphors, similes and onomatopoeia
- Give their opinion on an aspect of the poem
- Write their own poem

Instead of presenting all of these tasks at once, you might initially ask students only to read the poem and identify similes, holding back the other tasks until later. This helps students focus, reduces cognitive overload and makes the lesson more manageable to guide effectively.

If diagrams are given that are too complex, consider adapting them by drawing a simpler version on the board.

Germane Load

If, as a temporary teacher, you take steps to reduce both intrinsic and extraneous load, students will have greater mental capacity to focus on germane load – the effort required to process and engage with the task at hand. If they are able to do this, they are more likely to remember something in the long term, which is our key goal as temporary teachers.

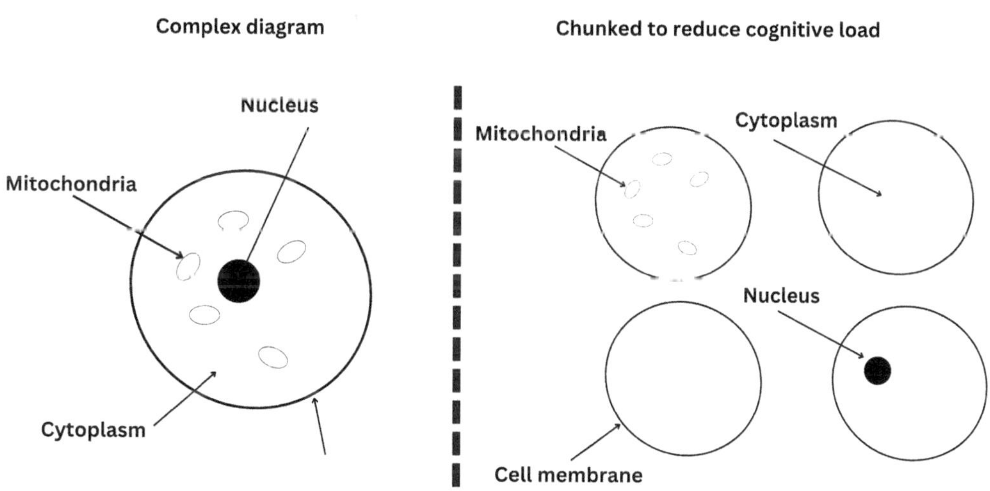

Figure 2.1 How to scaffold a diagram of a cell.

2.4 The Role of Schemas

Schemas are cognitive frameworks that help us organise and interpret information. They are built in long-term memory through repeated experiences and learning, allowing us to recognise patterns, make predictions and apply prior knowledge to new situations. Rather than storing isolated facts, schemas group related concepts together, which reduces the cognitive load on working memory by providing ready-made mental structures for processing new information.

The concept of the schema was first introduced by the psychologist Frederic Bartlett (1932) in his book *Remembering*. Bartlett's research showed that memory is not a perfect recording of events but is instead shaped by the mental frameworks we already hold. In his famous 'War of the Ghosts' experiment, British participants were asked to read and recall a Native American folk tale. Over time, their retellings became shorter, less detailed and subtly altered – details that didn't fit their cultural expectations were omitted or changed. For example, supernatural elements were often dropped, and unfamiliar references were replaced with ones that made sense within the participants' own cultural context. Bartlett argued that this happened because people interpret and reconstruct memories using their pre-existing schemas, filtering and reshaping information to fit what they already know.

Building on this foundation, Jean Piaget (1952) expanded the idea of schemas within his theory of cognitive development. For Piaget, schemas were not just passive memory frameworks but active mental structures that children use to understand and interact with the world. He described two key processes:

- *Assimilation* – fitting new experiences into existing schemas (e.g., a child who knows about dogs might call a cat a 'dog' at first, because it fits their existing framework of a four-legged animal).
- *Accommodation* – adjusting or creating new schemas when existing ones don't fit (the child realises cats are different from dogs and develops a new category).

Through assimilation and accommodation, Piaget argued, children gradually build more sophisticated schemas, driving their intellectual growth.

Together, Bartlett and Piaget's contributions show two sides of schemas: Bartlett highlighted how they shape memory and interpretation, while Piaget emphasised their role in development and learning. Modern educational psychology draws on both perspectives, recognising schemas as the essential mental structures that reduce cognitive load and enable transfer of knowledge.

The importance of activating schemas for comprehension was powerfully demonstrated by Bransford and Johnson (1972). In their experiment, participants were asked to listen to a short, deliberately vague passage. When read without context, most people found the passage confusing and struggled to recall its details. However, when others were told beforehand that the passage described 'doing laundry', their comprehension and memory improved dramatically. With the schema of 'laundry' activated, the same information suddenly made sense: Words like *clothes*, *washing*, *drying*, and *sorting* could be organised within an existing mental framework. The study showed that prior knowledge is not just helpful but essential – without a schema to connect new material to, working memory is overloaded, and learning breaks down.

Another crucial factor in building effective schemas is the way information is organised. Random, unstructured information places a heavy burden on working memory, making it harder to encode into long-term memory. In contrast, when knowledge is arranged into meaningful structures, it provides a scaffold for schema development.

Bower, Clark, Lesgold and Winzenz (1969) demonstrated this powerfully in an experiment in which participants were asked to learn lists of words. One group received the words in random order, while another was shown the same words arranged in a hierarchical structure, such as categories and subcategories. The results showed that those given the organised lists recalled nearly 90% of the words, compared to only 40% for those given unstructured lists. Simply having information presented in an organised way almost doubled memory performance.

This finding is echoed by Mandler (1967), who found that even without deliberate rehearsal, participants who organised information into categories remembered far more than those who did not. The act of organising itself, by highlighting relationships between ideas, strengthened memory traces and schema formation.

Application of Theory

Activating Schema

With experience, temporary teachers become better at judging how long it will take students to complete the content of a lesson plan. If it looks like you may need to find an additional task to fill time meaningfully, a simple strategy is to use the lesson title as a starting point. Ask students to spend five minutes writing down everything they already know about the topic.

For example:

- *History*: If the lesson title is 'The Causes of World War II', students might jot down key figures (Hitler, Chamberlain), events (Treaty of Versailles, appeasement), or broader ideas (economic depression, nationalism).
- *English*: If the lesson title is 'Exploring War Poetry', students might write what they know about poetry features (imagery, rhyme, stanza), or about war itself, such as feelings of fear, loss or patriotism.

This quick activity activates prior knowledge, helps you gauge what students already understand and provides a useful platform for discussion or questioning if you need to extend the lesson.

One of the temporary teachers I interviewed while preparing this book was Beth Hawkes from North Carolina. Beth works across high school and in a variety of subjects, often stepping in with little prior knowledge of the students or the curriculum. During our conversation, we explored strategies temporary teachers can use to enhance student learning, even in these challenging and unpredictable environments. Inspired by our discussion, Beth agreed to implement one of these techniques in her classrooms over several weeks. The following case study shares her experiences, showing not only the practical challenges of teaching in unfamiliar settings but also the ways in which thoughtful strategies can make a real difference for both students and teachers.

A Substitute Teacher's Guide to Activating Schemas – Beth Hawkes

I was a middle and high school science teacher for 25 years, 21 of them at the same school.

Now that I have 'retired' from the full-time classroom and am substituting 1–2 times per week in that school, I rarely get to teach in the same way I used to. If I sub for the physics teacher, I get to teach a full lesson, but that is rare. I am often in classes where I have little to no content knowledge. I might be in a Spanish class on Monday, a math class on Friday and a history class the following week.

But I'd still like to bring my knowledge and skills as an experienced teacher into the room to benefit the students in front of me. One thing that crosses all subject areas is retrieval practice. So, when it is appropriate, I begin the class by asking students to take out a blank sheet of paper and spend three minutes writing anything they remember learning from the previous week.

In doing this, I have found that I need to be flexible. There are times when it is difficult to implement. For example, I was subbing in a math class on the day of the homecoming pep rally, and the schedule had been adjusted, making classes ten minutes shorter than normal. I wasn't going to take three more of those minutes with a brain bomb, because they might not finish what the teacher had left for them to do. When I subbed in an art class, the nature of their routine was to come in, retrieve their supplies and start work on their projects right away.

It wouldn't have made sense for me to disrupt that routine with this kind of writing activity. There are also times when it just isn't appropriate to what the teachers have left, and I want to be respectful of that. One day in Spanish, for example, the students in two of the classes were already starting class with a journal assignment, so it didn't make sense to have those classes write again, so I only did brain bombs with the other classes she taught that day. A calculus teacher left tests for the students to take, and a theatre teacher left scenes for them to rehearse. Neither of those scenarios would have lent themselves well to a retrieval activity beforehand.

I think it is a case where a sub should use their own professional judgment about what is best on any given day. If you have knowledge of the science of learning, you can adapt it to a variety of situations and decide when it is best to employ those sorts of activities. I leave these brain bombs for the teacher so he or she can do anything they would like with it, and it is nice to know that I am helping students firm up their memory and activate their prior knowledge for the new lesson. I have gotten text messages from the teachers whose classes I have done it with, saying that they really appreciated having them. They got to see what their students remembered from the previous lesson, so it was a small act of formative assessment for them. It is my goal to help both the students and the teacher, and this is one small way I can do that.

What is key in Beth's example is her ability to adapt. As an experienced temporary teacher, she understands when to use a particular strategy and when it might not be appropriate. That's the goal of this chapter: To provide you with a range of strategies that support learning, so that over time you can build up a bank of approaches that work in different contexts. One of the advantages of temporary teaching is that if an attempt to introduce something new doesn't work, it matters less than it might for a permanent teacher – you can reflect, refine and try again with another class or in another school.

Organising Ideas

If you ask students to jot down what they learned in today's lesson, their natural tendency is often to write a short summary paragraph or a list of bullet points. While this can be useful, if our goal is to increase the likelihood of long-term retention, we can take it a step further by guiding students to organise their ideas more clearly and meaningfully.

Think about your own memory storage. If you are a football fan, whether that is American football or soccer, when asked to recall the players in your favourite team, you probably do not remember them as a random list of names. Instead, you visualise the team in formation and recall the players one by one in order. This shows how memory is strengthened when information is organised meaningfully rather than stored in isolation.

As a temporary teacher, you may find that the class teacher has left instructions for students to recap their learning at the end of the lesson, or you might decide to do this yourself if you run out of material. In either case, it is worth considering not just what students recall, but how they organise that knowledge.

For example:

- In a history class, if students are studying the suffragette movement, you could ask them to note key events in a timeline, helping them see cause and effect over time.
- In an English class, if they are reading a chapter from a novel, you might ask them to use a Venn diagram to compare the characteristics of two characters, highlighting similarities and differences.

- In a geography class, if they are learning about the causes of climate change, a mind map could help students connect natural causes, human activity and consequences, making relationships visible.
- In a biology class, if the topic is the classification of living organisms, you could ask students to create a hierarchical structure, such as kingdom, phylum, class, order, family, genus and species, to show how knowledge is systematically organised.

By nudging students toward different ways of structuring their recap, you help them build stronger schemas, mental frameworks that not only store knowledge but also make it easier to retrieve and apply in the future.

2.5 Retrieval Practice

Retrieval practice is the process of deliberately recalling information from memory rather than simply reviewing it. When students retrieve knowledge, they are actively pulling it from long-term memory into working memory. This strengthens the memory trace and reinforces the connections between pieces of knowledge, making it easier to recall in the future. In other words, retrieval practice doesn't just assess what students know – it changes the memory itself, enhancing its durability and accessibility.

Instead of re-reading notes or highlighting a text, students are asked to bring knowledge to mind, whether through low-stakes quizzes, questioning, flashcards or even writing down everything they can remember about a topic. By repeatedly activating and reconstructing information in working memory, students create stronger, more integrated schemas in long-term memory.

This principle has been demonstrated consistently in research. One of the most influential studies was carried out by Roediger and Karpicke (2006). They compared two groups of students who studied a passage of text. One group spent more time re-reading, while the other group studied and then completed recall tests. When tested a week later, the students who had practised retrieval remembered significantly more than those who had simply re-read the passage, despite having spent less overall time studying.

More recently, Agarwal, Bain and Chamberlain (2012) examined retrieval practice in real classrooms. They found that regular low-stakes quizzing not only improved test performance but also boosted long-term retention and student engagement. Importantly, the benefits of retrieval practice were strongest when quizzes were spaced out over time rather than crammed together, reinforcing the link between retrieval and spacing.

The evidence is clear: retrieval practice is not just a way of checking what students know, but one of the most effective ways to help them learn. By requiring knowledge to be recalled, it strengthens the connections in long-term memory, making future retrieval faster and more reliable.

Application of Theory

Brain Bomb

Earlier in the chapter, a strategy called *brain bomb* was introduced as a way of activating students' existing schema. This technique, illustrated through Beth Hawkes's case study, asks students to write down everything they can remember about a topic before new learning begins. While it holds value for developing students' schema, the brain bomb also serves another powerful function: It is a highly effective form of retrieval practice.

For a temporary teacher in particular, the brain bomb provides one of the quickest and most reliable ways to prompt students to retrieve what they already know, making their thinking visible and ready to be built upon.

This could be done at the start of a lesson, as suggested previously:

> Without looking at your notes, write down everything you can remember from the last lesson.

However, this could also be used at different key points in the lesson – for example, after watching a video or reading a text:

> Write down everything you can remember from the video.

It's important to distinguish this from activities that involve organising ideas. The goal of a brain bomb is not to carefully structure knowledge, but to recall as much information as possible in a short amount of time.

Think of memory practice like a fitness routine. Brain bombs are like sprint intervals: high-intensity bursts of effort that push your brain to retrieve as much information as possible. The focus is on speed and volume rather than perfect form, building raw recall power and stamina.

Organising ideas, on the other hand, is like weight training: controlled, deliberate practice that strengthens connections between pieces of knowledge. Here, students carefully structure, sequence and link ideas, building 'muscle memory' for understanding patterns and relationships.

Just like in a balanced fitness program, both brain bombs and organising ideas are necessary. Sprinting alone makes you fast but uncoordinated; lifting weights alone builds strength but not agility. Similarly, brain bombs improve the speed and quantity of recall, while organising ideas ensures that this knowledge is meaningful, interconnected and easier to retrieve in the future. Together, they create a strong, flexible and resilient memory.

Mini Quizzes

Research shows that mini quizzes are a highly effective form of retrieval practice. One simple way for temporary teachers to use this is to look through a student's book and identify a quiz or set of questions that was completed in the past few weeks. If some students finish their work early, you can copy these questions and ask them to complete the quiz again – without looking back at their notes or books.

Similarly, if students have finished the tasks set for the lesson, you can have them work in pairs to create their own mini quizzes based on the text. They can then test each other, reinforcing their understanding while actively retrieving information from memory.

Reduced Copying

The lesson plan you have been given may ask students to copy certain key pieces of information into their books for future reference. I would always follow the instructions the teacher has left for me; however, this doesn't stop you from increasing the challenge in the lesson.

For example, in geography, the teacher may want students to copy a diagram of the water cycle into their books, showing processes such as evaporation, condensation, precipitation and collection. Rather than copying it straight away, you could first ask students to study the diagram for five minutes and then draw the water cycle from memory, including as many processes as they can recall. This encourages them to retrieve multiple connected pieces of information at once, strengthening their understanding of the relationships between each stage before they see the correct diagram.

Here is a case study on how to implement this in your classroom from Adam Robbins, teacher, author and organiser of CogSciSci, a yearly conference aimed at sharing cognitive science amongst science teachers.

From Copying to Thinking: Transforming a Low-Demand Task into Learning – Adam Robbins

When I cover a class, I never know what I'll find on the desk. Sometimes it's a beautifully planned lesson with clear routines. Other times it's a set of slides and an instruction to 'get them to copy the notes'.

That was the case one Tuesday morning. The teacher was off sick, and Year 9 students were due to start a topic on emerging economies. The slides corresponding to the first activity were simple: A list of the BRICS countries with them marked on a map. All the students were expected to do is copy them into their books and then complete some short questions before moving on to the MINT countries in the next activity. No doubt the students would have been able to complete this task in a few minutes, but will they really think hard enough to begin to learn this important information?

I've never been a fan of copying as a teaching strategy. It looks productive, and it keeps students quiet, but the learning is surface level. Copying gives the illusion of work, not the substance of it. So, instead of following the plan exactly, I decided to make a few small adjustments that would keep the focus on thinking rather than transcription.

How can we turn a simple task like this into a productive learning experience?

1. *Animations.* The key strategy is to control the flow of information. I quickly animated the text on the slide, so it came up one at a time.
2. *Introduce the topic and the technique.* 'Right, then, year 9, listen carefully. I am going to teach you about emerging economies. Emerging economies are economies that are moving from being a less developed country to a developed industrialised country at a very fast rate. The map on the board shows these countries [gestures to board]. When I explain each part, I'm going to need you to listen carefully. I will ask you questions that are easy to answer if you have been listening. Each successful answer will get an achievement point to show my appreciation'.
3. *Deliver the information verbally to the class.* In this case I gestured to the first BRICS country (Brazil) and told the students, 'The first country is Brazil'.
4. *Pose the question to the class.* Say the question first, then pick a student to answer after a pause. This way all students think they might be called on and must think about the answer. 'What is the first emerging economy … Steven?' Notice the question is incredibly easy. I just want to trigger the thought of the information.

   'The first emerging economy is Brazil, sir', Steven replies.

   'Excellent listening Steven, point for you!'
5. I then clicked on the slide to reveal the word *Brazil* and began to point and identify the second country (Russia), Following a similar pattern.
6. Once all the BRICS countries have been identified I finished by highlighting that an easy way to remember them all is to recall the word 'brics' as it has the first letter of each country in it. 'What word has the first letter of every emerging economy in … Nafisa?
7. If the room, I was in had had mini-whiteboards, I may have then quizzed the students on the names of the BRICS countries. Instead, I asked them to turn and talk to their partner. 'When I say go and not before you are going to turn to your partner and try to remember all the BRICS countries …30 seconds, ready, go!' The aim is for them to rehearse their ideas and try some low stakes retrieval.
8. While they were talking, I wrote the sentence starter: 'The emerging economies are called the ______________; they include …' Once I had them silent, I instructed them to copy the sentence starter and complete it in silence. This independent work has taken the place of the copying. It has taken longer to get to this point, but the work they are producing is a product of their own thinking, so I am confident there is a better chance of their remembering the BRICS nations for the rest of the lesson.
9. Before moving on I need to ensure the students have seen the correct answer. I ask a student to read out their answer and show the slide a final time.

The key thing for me is to consider how I can try to make the students active participants at each stage in the lesson and drive their thinking towards the lesson's objectives.

2.6 Dual Coding

The concept of dual coding was first proposed by Allan Paivio in the 1970s. He argued that human cognition relies on two distinct but interconnected mental systems: One for processing verbal information, and one for processing non-verbal, visual information. Paivio's experiments demonstrated that information encoded in both systems is more easily retrieved than information encoded in only one. For example, when learning a new concept in science, pairing a diagram with an explanation does more than simply provide extra context; it allows students to form multiple pathways in memory, creating a richer, more flexible mental representation of the concept. This dual representation not only improves recall but also enhances understanding, as students can draw on both the verbal and visual elements to solve problems, make connections and apply knowledge in new contexts.

Research since then has supported the effectiveness of dual coding across subjects and ages (Paivio, 1971; Wooten & Cuevas, 2024). Studies show that combining text and visuals can:

- Increase recall and comprehension.
- Reduce cognitive load by giving students multiple ways to process information.
- Help learners build stronger connections between ideas.

Application of Theory

In practice, dual coding can be as simple as pairing a labelled diagram with notes, creating timelines with images or summarising a concept using both words and pictures. So if you have spare time in the lesson, consider getting students to create an image or images to represent what they have learnt.

Subject	Concept	Text Example	Visual Example
Geography	River erosion and deposition	'Rivers erode the banks in their upper course and deposit sediment in the lower course'.	Diagram of a river with arrows showing erosion, transport and deposition zones.
English	Character development	'The protagonist becomes more confident as the story progresses'.	Character arc graph or comic strip showing key events and changes.

(Continued)

Subject	Concept	Text Example	Visual Example
Maths	Pythagoras' theorem	'In a right-angled triangle, the square of the hypotenuse equals the sum of the squares of the other two sides'.	Triangle diagram with squares on each side labelled $a^2 + b^2 = c^2$
Science	States of matter	'Solids have fixed shape and volume, liquids have fixed volume but change shape, gases change shape and volume'.	Diagram showing molecules in solid, liquid, and gas states.
History	Industrial Revolution	'The Industrial Revolution led to urbanisation and new manufacturing processes'.	Timeline with key inventions, factories and population growth visuals.
Art	Colour theory	'Complementary colours create strong contrast and harmony'.	Colour wheel highlighting complementary pairs.
Languages	Verb conjugation (Spanish)	'Yo hablo, tú ablas, él/ella habla'.	Table of verb endings alongside stick-figure illustrations of actions.
PE	Muscle groups	'The biceps contract to flex the arm, triceps contract to extend it'.	Diagram of arm with biceps/triceps labelled and arrows showing movement.

2.7 Equity for All

The last section of this chapter focuses not on discrete teaching techniques based on our understanding of cognitive science, but instead on overarching principles that are evidenced informed.

Temporary teachers face many challenges when they do not know their students. Perhaps the most significant is not being aware of their starting points. This idea was captured clearly by David Ausubel, who argued that "the most important single factor influencing learning is what the learner already knows. Ascertain this and teach him accordingly" (Ausubel, 1968, p. 18).

Teachers may not consciously be thinking about this precise phrase when setting cover work, but it explains why so much of what is left for absent teachers to deliver involves recap rather than new learning. Repeating material that students are assumed to already know feels safer when you are unsure of their understanding. However, when a teacher's absence lasts longer than a few days, it becomes impossible to continue relying on revision alone. At some point, decisions have to be made about moving forward with the curriculum.

Earlier in the book I introduced a case study from Alex Fairlamb, who shared her experiences as a cover teacher early in her career. When I was thinking about how to promote equity in lessons taught by a temporary teacher, she was the first person I contacted. Alex is the co-author of the excellent book *The Scaffolding Effect* (Ball & Fairlamb, 2025), which is built on a powerful premise: students should not be given different work based on perceived ability – *Johnny, you're not very good at maths, so you take the easy worksheet* – but should instead be supported so that everyone can reach the same endpoint, even if some require more help along the way.

Many of the strategies in *The Scaffolding Effect* rely on skilled teachers being able to diagnose precisely where each student is in their understanding and to provide tailored support in response. For a temporary teacher, however, this is rarely possible. There is simply not enough time to plan the right questions and extract the rich information needed to make those judgements.

So I asked Alex to apply her expertise to a different problem: how might a temporary teacher provide effective scaffolding for students without knowing their starting points? What follows is the advice she shared with me.

Scaffolding Without a Safety Net: Supporting Learning in Short- and Long-Term Temporary Teaching Roles – Alex Fairlamb

A supply teacher typically (but not always) falls into two categories: short term (day by day, varied subjects beyond your specialism) and medium to long term (usually a week or longer, usually – but not always – within your specialism) This case study discusses both scenarios with regard to what practical scaffolding strategies can be utilised to create the conditions which will help students to be successful in your lesson.

Short-Term Supply Teaching Scaffolding Strategies

In most situations, in a singular day or a few days' supply employment, you are unlikely to receive detailed information about the students you're teaching. Typically, a seating plan with some key notes about Education, Health and Care Plans (EHCPs) or Pupil Premium (PP) may be left. However, rich data such as reading ages and attendance won't always be available due to the short-term nature of the employment and the time with which to process the information, particularly if moving across multiple classes, classrooms and subjects within a day.

So what scaffolding strategies can be used when scant information is available/able to be processed and you have two minutes before 30 students enter the classroom you walked into one minute earlier? The following outlines four key strategies:

- *Reading.* If a lesson requires students to read a textbook, an extract or pages from a textbook or a book/text, I recommend using teacher-led modelled reading. In teacher-led modelled reading, using strategies such as reciprocal reading (asking students to turn and talk to summarise key lines or explicitly teaching key words) means that you can model the prosody, intonation and fluency of a strategic reader. Rather than risking the chance that students may be able to access the text and therefore the subsequent tasks relating to it, or asking students (whose reading ages you might not know) to read aloud as directed by instructions, this provides an opportunity to scaffold reading and check for understanding to be able to adapt the instructions left to either explain further key words or clarify things. Additionally, if the lesson you are covering is in your discipline, you can re-teach or provide knowledge to secure learning.
- *Videos.* When playing videos, activate the subtitles, pause the video to allow for processing and discussion time, and play it twice. Often we expect them to watch a video once and know the key detail, but playing it twice gives the opportunity to watch and process the information, then watch and apply to questions. This helps to reduce the split-attention effect, as you're avoiding asking them to listen, watch and write simultaneously.
- *Chunking the explanation of tasks and content.* As a previous cover supervisor, I made the error of stating all three to five tasks that the students needed to do and then expecting them to work methodically through them. What works better is to create a chunked, timed sequence of tasks with checks for understanding which include asking (in an inclusive way): What do we need to do? What knowledge do you have to apply to this? Clarify for me what your task is.
- *Verbal nudges.* Often we consider scaffolding to be written. However, verbal is an effective strategy to use, particularly as a supply teacher. Asking, 'What did you do the last time you answered this question?', 'What is the success criteria you usually use?' or 'Where can you access the core knowledge you need for this question?' results in students thinking deeply about what they may already know or where to access existing scaffolds to use.

Medium- and Longer-Term Supply Teaching Scaffolding Strategies

Typically, in these situations it will be more likely that you'll have access to data which can support planning scaffolds by anticipating the barriers. Additionally, your growing knowledge of the students and their day-to-day experiences and your formative and summative assessment means that you'll additionally be able to anticipate barriers and be responsive in a way that short-term supply teachers don't have the opportunity to be. Much of the medium- and long-term supply teaching employment will involve using typical scaffolding strategies, as outlined in *The Scaffolding Effect* (Ball & Fairlamb, 2025).

That said, there can sometimes be school/trust-set ways of working, including lesson structure and how homework is set, which may make the following advice variable in terms of potential to implement. Each context is different.

With the medium- and long-term nature of the engagement with students, the following four areas are key things to focus upon:

- *Creating a preliminary understanding knowledge check.* Using the departmental long-term plans and progression model, create a cumulative knowledge check that helps you to determine which aspects of prior knowledge are secure. An example is within history, it would be difficult to teach the reasons for war in 1939 if students weren't secure on the implications of the Treaty of Versailles and its impact in Germany, the NSDAP rhetoric from 1919 onwards regarding this treaty and the resulting steps taken to dismantle it during the 1930s. By creating a knowledge check, you can determine where key concepts need to be revisited or strengthened and what core knowledge needs consolidation.
- *The aforementioned reading strategy if not an English or MFL subject.* The curriculum time dedicated to subjects that aren't 'core' means we cannot run the risk of deploying independent reading or have the time for echo reading. As someone who has experienced 55-minute-a-week lessons dedicated to my subject or two hours in a week at GCSE, time means using the most high-leverage strategies during a finite amount of time. Reciprocal reading means frequent checks for understanding, and it creates the conditions for adaptations that may not be visible with independent or echo reading (where students repeat a short section of text after the teacher, allowing all learners to access complex material by borrowing the fluency and phrasing of an expert reader).
- *Aide-mémoires.* Using aide-mémoires, such as knowledge organisers, writing frames and subject-specific tools such as timelines, key quotes from *An Inspector Calls* or case studies in geography or psychology, can support students when digesting new reading and information, applying knowledge to questions or carrying out practice questions. These can be invaluable when implemented well.
- *Visualiser use.* Using a visualiser means that you can model strategic reading by annotating a text as you unpick it via reciprocal reading, interrogating success criteria against two comparative answers or using it to model answering a question. You can live-model or use examples of effective work for students to adjust their own thinking and work, and you can demonstrate internal thinking (what, how, why) which can help students to better underhand the mechanisms of a process.

One major advantage of being a temporary teacher is that you get to see a wide range of high-quality resources in action. As Alex has suggested, providing students with aide-mémoires can be a powerful scaffold, enabling them to access the lesson even when their prior knowledge is uncertain. When you cover a lesson that uses an especially effective resource, it is worth keeping a copy for yourself.

However I would also encourage you, when leaving notes for the class teacher, to mention that you found the resource particularly useful and that you hope they do not mind your taking a copy. Teaching is, by nature, a sharing profession – we all want the best for students – but professional courtesy still matters.

Over time, you will build up a small collection of resources that are so valuable you will take them with you whenever you are covering.

2.8 Why Oracy Matters

When you walk into a classroom as a temporary teacher, you are often handed a worksheet, a seating plan, and the unspoken expectation that your job is simply to keep students quiet and get through the hour. In those moments, talk can feel like the enemy. Noise equals risk. Discussion equals loss of control. Silence, on the other hand, feels safe.

But that instinct, understandable as it is, works against how learning actually happens.

Oracy, the ability to express ideas clearly, listen to others and build meaning through talk, is far more than 'just speaking'. Research shows that oral language development is one of the strongest predictors of long-term academic success, with early oral proficiency linked to later attainment across subjects (National Literacy Trust, 2018; Snow, 2010). Structured classroom discussion helps students deepen understanding, build vocabulary and develop reasoning skills in ways that go beyond memorising facts for a test – *it creates learning* (Alexander, 2008; Mercer & Littleton, 2007).

Classroom talk that is genuinely dialogic, where students are invited to explain, justify and connect ideas, has been shown to correlate with higher student achievement compared to predominantly teacher-led discussion (Waitoller & Kozleski, 2013). When students articulate their thinking, they are more likely to notice gaps in their understanding, make connections between concepts and retain knowledge over time.

The benefits of oracy extend even further than academic outcomes. Evidence suggests that talk-rich classrooms help foster confidence, engagement and social development and can play a role in narrowing attainment gaps, especially for learners from disadvantaged backgrounds (Education Endowment Foundation, 2018; My Chartered College, 2020).

This matters deeply for temporary teachers. Even in a single lesson, the way you invite students to speak, explain, question and listen can transform the learning climate. It can turn a passive cover lesson into a space where thinking happens and where students feel *seen* and *heard*. You don't need to be in a school for a term to shape how a student experiences learning – you just need to give them permission, and structure, to use their voice.

Oracy isn't an add-on. It is the bridge between what students think and what they understand, and it is one of the most powerful tools you have as a temporary teacher.

With this in mind, I turned to Nikki Sullivan, the co-author of a brilliant book called *Unlocking Oracy*. As with other case studies in this book, I asked her to apply her expertise to supporting temporary teachers to give them to tools to promote oracy in their classrooms.

Purposeful Talk: Using Oracy to Support Learning in the Supply Classroom – Nikki Sullivan: Co-Author, *Unlocking Oracy*, Deputy Headteacher, and Trust CPD Programmes Lead

One understandable concern surrounding oracy is that student talk might shift from purposeful, learning-focused discourse to off-task chatter. Nevertheless, studies, such as that from Sedova and Sedlacek (2023), highlight the importance of utilising strategies that lean upon student talk, enabling contributions from all learners, if we are to accelerate learning.

In the supply classroom, the desire to accelerate learning remains. Additionally, the learning problems teachers face – securing attention, supporting students to think hard and make meaning, strengthening memory – are the same.

Based on the challenges of supply teaching highlighted to me, here are some strategies which utilise oracy not only to support learning, but to overcome barriers faced by teachers who have not planned the lessons they are delivering.

Strengthening the Start

The start of a lesson sets the tone. Should a supply teacher find themselves unable to immediately locate the cover work, this not only results in lost learning time, but also has a knock-on effect on classroom culture. Establish one topic that the class has recently been studying and ask students to silently brain dump (on a mini-whiteboard should they be readily available, or on paper, or in the back of their books as needed) everything they can remember about that topic. Explaining to students that this act of retrieval helps strengthen memory can support engagement. Asking students to come up with 'at least X' number of ideas helps push students to challenge themselves.

Students can then be allocated a partner – usually the person they share a desk with, as opposed to students moving around the room. Students can then act as learning resources for one another (Wiliam, 2011) and compare their notes, starting to group pieces of information that they have retrieved where possible. As students discuss what they have written down, they are comparing their own external memory field (Donald, 1991) with their partner's, seeing what they had missed, but also grappling with whether two points, written differently but appearing to refer to the same idea, are indeed the same; and if so, which is more clear.

Once students have pulled together their thinking, they can be set one final challenge of condensing their thinking into what they perceive to be the ten most salient pieces of information. Of course, the subject lens here is key (the above strategy may not be as successful in mathematics; depending on the age of the learners, a task linked to timetables, multiples, factors, products of primes, etc., may be more fruitful). Considering what information is 'most important' as a supply teacher can be a challenge, as we are unlikely to be equally equipped to determine what is 'need-to-know' versus 'neat-to-know' information (Tomsett, 2023; Wiliam, 2022) in all subjects. Nevertheless, getting students to 'think hard' in this way, needing to determine what to include and what to exclude in their summary, can strengthen prior learning.

Crucially, there must be an appropriate checking mechanism in place. Where possible, students need to be able to refer back to their work in their learning resources (exercise books, knowledge organisers, etc.) in order that any information retrieved which is incorrect can be amended by the students.

Strengthening the Use of Text

Where extended texts form a significant part of the cover material which has been left for the class, there are multiple ways to approach the reading of this text. Strategies such as Lemov's (2021) FASE reading help to secure class attention as students follow the text with a finger or ruler and need to be ready to take over the reading when their name is called. Where reading aloud is not already established as a norm, attention can still be secured by using simple cold call or choral response questioning to rehearse key pieces of information from the text. As the teacher reads aloud, they can get to the end of a short section and ask, 'What is the name of reactions where oxygen is removed?', before selecting a student to respond or indicating that the class should respond, resulting in the individual or the class restating 'Reduction reactions'. This simple rehearsal of information may not be the hard thinking that is required to move information into long-term memory, but students' attention has been secured through the way in which they are either reading the text aloud or needing to be ready to respond to rehearsal questions – and we know that attention is the 'gatekeeper of our WM [working memory]' (McCrea, 2017, p. 39).

Where there are concerns that the amount of work that has been left may not last a whole lesson, or resources cannot be found, students can be asked to summarise each paragraph or short section. Although this could be completed as a written task, it can also be completed verbally. The routine should be established that after each person in the pair has completed their summary, their partner who is listening has to add at least one additional point, thereby strengthening the attention of the listening partner on what their partner is saying. Students can then move on from this verbal rehearsal to summarising each paragraph in writing, having had the opportunity to thrash around their thinking before writing down these more final thoughts.

Strengthening Memory

In *Unlocking Oracy* (Sullivan, Heaton & Lowde, 2025), Alex Quigley discusses a strategy which he calls 'Just a Minute'. This strategy involves students talking about a topic for a minute without stopping, providing an opportunity for students to engage in resource-free, purposeful oracy activity, where students are explaining and elaborating – thinking hard and, therefore, strengthening their learning about that particular topic. It may well be that certain students come to the front to complete their minute. However, this strategy can work in pairs, whereby, once again, the listening partner has a key role in feeding back to their partner, not on the quality of their presentation but with any questions or clarifications they may have based on their understanding of the learning material. The teacher sets the timer and observes and circulates to support the climate for learning, leaving an additional 60 seconds for the feedback or follow-up questions, before students swap roles. This strategy can be completed for the topic and text which has been explored in the lesson, but can also be utilised as a revision strategy for previous topics where additional time within the lesson is available.

To Close

We know that oracy can strengthen learning. In the supply classroom, purposeful activities which lean upon speaking and listening must be carefully structured in order to secure attention and create a purposeful climate for learning where all learners contribute. Where these foundations are established, not only can we support students' learning, but we can also create a buzz of learning-focused talk as part of our classroom toolkit.

2.9 Metacognition

Metacognition refers to the awareness and control of one's own thinking and learning processes. In simpler terms, it is 'thinking about thinking'. It involves planning how to approach a task, monitoring comprehension and progress while working and evaluating the effectiveness of strategies once a task is completed. By developing metacognitive skills, students can become more independent learners, being better able to identify what they know, what they don't and how best to bridge that gap.

I begin with a case study from Nathan Burns, author of two books on metacognition. I asked Nathan to identify three metacognitive strategies that could be implemented widely and sustainably in classrooms, regardless of subject or age group. His responses focus not on bolt-on activities, but on practices that can be embedded into everyday teaching to help pupils become more aware of how they learn, not just what they learn.

Developing Metacognition in the Cover Classroom: A Universal Set of Beneficial Approaches – Nathan Burns

Too often in lesson, students 'go through the motions', copying examples from the board, meandering through a worksheet or 'don't know-ing' their way through teacher questioning. This issue is only exacerbated within a one-off cover lesson, where the work set can be limited, shallow in the thinking that it causes, and made all the more difficult where you as the cover teacher do not know the students, and the students do not know you.

'To be metacognitive' is to think deeply. Acts of evaluating strengths and areas for improvement, and considerations as to how knowledge builds and link together, are all examples of effective metacognitive thought. But perhaps none of these thoughts appear all too possible in a cover lesson, which is unfortunate – being metacognitive in our learning can, after all, accelerate learning by a whopping eight months every single year (Education Endowment Foundation, n.d.).

Now, despite the challenges, either with the work being left or our own subject knowledge, there are in fact several approaches that we can take in the classroom to orchestrate effective metacognitive thinking, at the drop of a hat.

A first approach well worth considering is the idea of a goal-free problem. Originally developed in the mathematics classroom as a response to longer-form problem questions, a goal-free problem can be adapted to suit any curriculum area and learning phase. The idea is simple. Wherever a longer-form problem or context problem is given (you know the ones – where there are graphs, tables, quotes, longer written prose and so forth), the question, right at the very end is simply … removed. But why would you do this? So often, with these sorts of multi-step questions, students can feel intimidated.

Where do they begin? What if they cannot do all of the steps? What if they cannot recall a specific fact or quote? It is so often easier to just not do the work, rather than just give it a go. But through removing the question, students are suddenly unshackled – and are free to work out, evaluate and deduce as many things as possible from the given context. A simply four-step maths question can be transformed into a 'low barrier, high ceiling' activity that students can be working on for the whole lesson, for example.

A second approach worth considering is the idea of Do It Again. Very often, cover work will constitute completing worksheets of recall topics that students ought to remember from previous weeks of teaching. On many occasions, students are allowed to work through these questions using any approach that they wish to. However, too often, this leads to limited thinking and students passively working through a set of questions. One way to break this up is to provide students with the answers (once they have done it the first time) and then get them to repeat the task/question a second time but using a different method. Through doing this, students need to actively consider alternative strategies and evaluate the effectiveness of these different approaches.

A final metacognitive approach centres around student self-determined evaluation. Once they have finished their given tasks, why not get students to note down the questions and/or topics that they struggled with? But beyond this, students could then make notes on how they could improve in these areas, and what precise questions they need to ask their teacher upon their return. These are simple questions and tasks to add in to any lesson but significantly support the development of student Independence.

I chose to share the use of metacognitive strategies, alongside Nathan Burns's case study, towards the end of this chapter for a reason. Goal-free tasks offer an opportunity to revisit and consolidate several key ideas from cognitive science that have already been explored in this book. Think of this section as a deliberate return to that core knowledge – an attempt to strengthen it through spaced revisiting, in the hope of increasing the likelihood that it is retained in your long-term memory as the reader.

At their heart, goal-free tasks are closely linked to CLT, most notably the work of John Sweller. Sweller identified that when learners – particularly novices – are given a clear end goal, their working memory is often consumed by trying to find a route to the answer. Rather than focusing on understanding the relationships within a problem, pupils engage in what Sweller (1988) termed means–ends analysis: constantly asking themselves how far they are from the finish and what step might get them closer.

This search for the answer places a significant burden on working memory. When too much mental effort is spent juggling possible methods, formulas or facts, there is little capacity left for learning to occur. For many pupils, this is the point at which confidence drops and task avoidance begins.

Consider a simple example from a mathematics classroom. A typical goal-driven question might read:

A car accelerates from rest at 2 m/s² for 5 seconds. Calculate the distance travelled.

For a novice learner, the cognitive demand here is high. They must recall the correct formula, decide which values to substitute, hold multiple pieces of information in working memory and monitor whether they are getting closer to the required answer. Much of their mental effort is spent *searching* for a solution rather than understanding the relationships between acceleration, time, velocity and distance.

A goal-free version of the same task might instead say:

A car accelerates from rest at 2 m/s² for 5 seconds. What can you work out from this information?

The cognitive experience for the student changes immediately. There is no single endpoint to reach and no sense of failure for not 'getting it all right'. One pupil may calculate the final velocity, another might work out the distance travelled, while others may identify relationships or explain how acceleration affects motion over time. Every valid deduction moves learning forward.

This is where schema building takes place. By reducing unnecessary cognitive load, goal-free tasks allow pupils to focus on making sense of the structure of the problem. They begin to see how quantities relate, how principles connect and why certain methods work. Over time, these connections are organised into schemas – mental frameworks that can be retrieved and applied flexibly in future problems.

For temporary teachers, this matters. A single goal-free task can become a genuinely low-barrier, high-ceiling activity: accessible to all, challenging for many and rich in thinking. More importantly, it shifts the purpose of the task away from merely producing an answer and towards building understanding that lasts.

Similarly, when Nathan refers to self-determined evaluation, this can be usefully connected to several ideas that have already been discussed in this chapter

Step 1: Plan

- *Action*: Decide how to tackle your task.
- *Ask*: What do I already know? What strategy will work best?
- *Example*: Before a history task on World War II, jot down key events you remember.

Step 2: Monitor

- *Action*: Check your understanding while working.
- *Ask*: Am I remembering correctly? Where am I stuck?
- *Example*: During a science brain dump on photosynthesis, notice steps you can't recall.

Step 3: Evaluate

- *Action*: Reflect on what worked and what didn't.
- *Ask*: What helped me? What should I do differently next time?
- *Example*: After making a geography mind map of rivers, check for missing features and add them in a different-coloured pen.

Step 4: Adjust/Improve

- *Action*: Change strategies for better results next time.
- *Ask*: How can I study differently to remember more?
- *Example*: Try a timeline instead of a list if it helps you recall history events more clearly.

2.10 The Most Challenging Subjects to Cover

When interviewing temporary teachers and from my own experience, two subjects consistently come up as the most challenging to cover: drama and languages. Each presents its own difficulties, but drama, in particular, can feel daunting for temporary teachers.

I still remember my first drama cover lesson. As usual, I began by lining the students up outside while I set up the computer and projector – something I discuss in more detail in the next chapter. I rushed to connect the HDMI cable and get the PowerPoint onto the board. In hindsight, I needn't have bothered. The slide simply read: *Plan a scene following the one you have been provided. Use the techniques you have been working on.* On the desk was a printed copy of the scene they were expected to read. I left it there and went to the door to greet the class.

Unlike a normal classroom, where I can stand at the door and still maintain visibility of the room, the layout of the drama studio made this almost impossible. Several pieces of staging blocked my line of sight. As the students disappeared into the large space one by one, the noise steadily rose. By the time I greeted the final student and stepped inside, I was met with a chaotic scene – 30 students scattered around the studio, some standing in clusters, some play-fighting, others running about.

I describe in the next chapter how I managed the situation and share a range of practical strategies to support temporary teachers who find themselves facing a similar challenge. Despite my best attempts to establish order, the lack of structure in the lesson made it feel as though I spent most of the hour playing a game of 'whack-a-mole'.

While the other case studies in this chapter focus on general classroom techniques, the next example comes from Richard Lynch, teacher of drama and teaching and learning team member at DESS College Dubai. He offers a set of clear structures that can help break a drama lesson into manageable chunks – reducing the likelihood of the challenging behaviour that so often emerges when students are given free rein in a large, echoing space.

Strategies to Make a Drama Cover Lesson Manageable, Engaging and Fun! – Richard Lynch

'Covering a drama lesson' – four words that notoriously strike fear into the hearts of the most experienced of teachers. Having taught secondary drama for over ten years, I've heard lessons described as chaotic and unstructured, leaving non-specialist teachers feeling unsure of how to keep students on task. The cover instructions are often carefully balanced between being vague enough for a non-specialist but specific enough to engage students. 'Work in groups to devise a scene' is all the instruction you have been given – the key is to break the task into clear timed chunks, giving responsibility, direction and small, measurable goals.

Step 1: Provide a Stimulus

Promote the students' creativity and support their independence by giving a simple stimulus. This could be a picture, a quote, a scenario such as 'the discovered bag' or 'the unexpected visitor'. This could also be an opportunity for you to bring in something from your own subject specialism or student/personal interests. Introducing a shared stimulus unites students with focus and supports those who lose motivation in the early stages as they are unsure how to start.

Step 2: Assign Group Roles

Distribute roles within each group to encourage accountability and aim for groups of three to keep it manageable.

- Student 1 – Director (keeps the group focused)
- Student 2 – Timekeeper (monitors deadlines)
- Student 3 – Recorder (notes ideas)

Hold students accountable to these roles through questioning at various points throughout the lesson.

Step 3: Planning the Scene

In the structured planning phase, pose three simple questions to promote their thinking and ownership: Who are the characters? What is the problem? How will it end? The questions can also be your checkpoints to measure students' engagement and progress.

Step 4: Rehearse with a Focus

Entitle each 10- to 15-minute rehearsal block with a particular focus, such as 'Establish the characters and the problem', 'Include a still image', 'Utilise slow motion as a technique' or 'Experiment with sound effects'. This keeps the groups concentrated on smaller achievable goals that can be measured.

Step 5: Keep It Short

Have all groups perform simultaneously. All students move into their starting positions with the only audience being you, allowing you to measure progress. Have students select their favourite part of their scene and limit them to 30–45 seconds of performance time. This strengthens students' evaluative skills as well as maintaining the pace of the lesson.

Step 6: Reflection

End the session with a short reflective discussion where you encourage students to link back to their assigned role or the rehearsal foci. 'What did you do well?' or 'Who impressed you today and why?'

If you are a non-specialist, consider keeping all the discussion positive as managing areas for development could require more subject knowledge. A reflective discussion gives the lesson a purposeful conclusion, makes the learning explicit and helps students stay on task until the school bell sounds.

In conclusion, chunking down a drama cover lesson into short, structured steps – stimulus, roles, planning, focused rehearsals, short performances and reflection – supports student engagement and cover teacher confidence. Adopt this approach for meaningful and manageable lessons that maximise learning and creativity so that next time you see the words 'Covering a drama lesson', your own stage fright won't set in.

The final case study in this chapter focuses on Spanish. The challenges of covering languages are not primarily related to the anxiety of large spaces or unstructured time; rather, they stem from the fact that, unless you speak the language, it can be difficult to adapt lessons or add meaningful value to students' learning experiences. To explore this further, I spoke with George Jack, a languages teacher and assistant head at Aiglon College, Switzerland, and asked him: How can temporary teachers enhance language lessons? The following case study conveys his suggestions.

Curating a Personal Linguistic Toolkit: Maximising Language Learning in Cover Lessons – George Jack

Sometimes in language teaching, we rush through curricula with little regard for spaced retrieval practice. Cover lessons can function as the perfect opportunity for students to stop, take stock of their linguistic development and consolidate their go-to vocabulary and sentence chunks for effective spontaneous production. If you have a world languages cover lesson, ask students to look back through their work and the textbook in order to note down useful vocabulary that they have encountered previously that will allow them to communicate effectively going forward. Ask them to create five different tables – adjectives, common verbs, nouns, intensifiers and 'stallers'. 'Stallers' is absolutely not a grammatical term, but they help students to pause in order to reflect and continue spontaneous production – think 'I would say that', or 'That's a good point'. Each table should be separated into columns that include 'Term', home language meaning and example of the term in action. For verbs, you need a high-frequency-conjugation section. For instance, the term could be the word 'to write'. There would be a home language meaning and the example of 'I write content for Richard Wheadon because he's a legend'.

Naturally, as we all would, students write the first ten things they see in their books. However, encouraging them to categorise the words from the outset encourages reflection and, to some extent, careful consideration. If you feel that students aren't taking the task seriously, you can ask them to either justify that the vocabulary is 'common' through asking them to provide multiple examples from their books or asking them to pair up and compare notes. You can capitalise on these pairs even more by asking students to teach each other the content in context (explaining the vocabulary and then giving some examples) so as to demonstrate mastery. In order to give the task meaning, you can emphasise that this is an excellent revision exercise given that students will have revisited the content that could and most probably will come up in assessments. It is important to circulate regularly and reinforce high expectations to ensure that the task is worthwhile. Some students then choose to perform this task at the end of every unit to contribute towards eventual knowledge organisers.

As the lesson concludes, it may be worth initiating a short discussion upon effective retrieval practice, the power of forgetting and the intervals at which it is useful to revisit content. This task is effective only when intrinsic motivation is maximised, and therefore, buy-in must be established at the beginning, reinforced throughout and then reiterated at the end. Ultimately, I feel that this task transforms a cover lesson into a powerful vehicle for student autonomy, which ensures that rather than simply filling time, we empower learners to curate a personalised linguistic toolkit necessary for long-term retention and genuine spontaneous fluency.

Conclusion

This chapter has shown how evidence-informed strategies from cognitive science can be seamlessly woven into everyday lessons, even when time is limited or the students are unfamiliar. By exploring techniques such as retrieval practice, dual coding, scaffolding, metacognition and purposeful oracy, the chapter highlights how temporary teachers can create strong routines that support learning, memory and independence. The wider examples and case studies illustrate that these approaches are not add-ons but practical, high-impact ways to strengthen thinking and understanding in the classroom. Ultimately, building these routines helps ensure every lesson, however brief, contributes meaningfully to students' progress and sets the stage for the next focus on behaviour and attitudes.

References

Agarwal, P. K., Bain, P. M., & Chamberlain, R. W. (2012). The value of applied research: Retrieval practice improves classroom learning and recommendations from a teacher, a principal, and a scientist. *Educational Psychology Review*, 24(3), 437–448. https://doi.org/10.1007/s10648-012-9210-2

Alexander, R. (2008). *Towards Dialogic Teaching: Rethinking Classroom Talk* (4th ed.). Cambridge, UK: Dialogos.

Ausubel, D. P. (1968). *Educational Psychology: A Cognitive View*. New York: Holt, Rinehart and Winston.

Ball, R., & Fairlamb, A. (2025). *The Scaffolding Effect: Supporting all Students to Succeed*. London: Routledge.

Bartlett, F. C. (1932). *Remembering: A Study in Experimental and Social Psychology*. Cambridge: Cambridge University Press.

Beck, I. L., McKeown, M. G., & Kucan, L. (2013). *Bringing Words to Life: Robust Vocabulary Instruction* (2nd ed.). New York: Guilford Press.

Bower, G. H., Clark, M. C., Lesgold, A. M., & Winzenz, D. (1969). Hierarchical retrieval schemes in recall of categorized word lists. *Journal of Verbal Learning and Verbal Behavior*, 8(3), 323–343.

Bransford, J. D., & Johnson, M. K. (1972). Contextual prerequisites for understanding: Some investigations of comprehension and recall. *Journal of Verbal Learning and Verbal Behavior*, 11(6), 717–726. https://doi.org/10.1016/S0022-5371(72)80006-9

Chartered College of Teaching. (2020). *The Impact of Oracy On Learning and Attainment.* London: Chartered College of Teaching. https://literacytrust.org.uk

Covey, S. R. (1989). *The 7 Habits of Highly Effective People: Powerful Lessons in Personal Change.* New York: Free Press.

Craik, F. I. M., & Tulving, E. (1975). Depth of processing and the retention of words in episodic memory. *Journal of Experimental Psychology: General,* 104(3), 268–294. https://doi.org/10.1037/0096-3445.104.3.268

Donald, M. (1991). *Origins of the Modern Mind: Three Stages in the Evolution of Culture and Cognition.* Cambridge, MA: Harvard University Press.

Education Endowment Foundation. (2018). *Improving Literacy in Secondary Schools: Guidance Report.* London: Education Endowment Foundation. https://educationendowmentfoundation.org.uk

Education Endowment Foundation. (n.d.). *Teaching and Learning Toolkit: Metacognition and Self-Regulation.* https://educationendowmentfoundation.org.uk/education-evidence/teaching-learning-toolkit/metacognition-and-self-regulation

Hughes, M. (2013). *The Magenta Principles: Choosing Action Over Comfort.* Carmarthen: Crown House Publishing.

Lemov, D. (2021). *Teach Like a Champion 3.0: 63 Techniques That Put Students on the Path to College.* 3rd ed. Newark, NJ: Jossey-Bass.

Mandler, G. (1967). Organization and memory. *Journal of Verbal Learning and Verbal Behavior,* 6(2), 175–195.

McCrea, P. (2017). *Memorable Teaching: Leveraging Memory to Build Deep and Durable Learning in the Classroom.* Woodbridge, UK: John Catt Educational.

Mercer, N., & Littleton, K. (2007). *Dialogue and the Development of Children's Thinking: A Sociocultural Approach.* London: Routledge.

Miller, G. A. (1956). The magical number seven, plus or minus two: Some limits on our capacity for processing information. *Psychological Review,* 63(2), 81–97. https://doi.org/10.1037/h0043158

Murdoch, B. B. (1962). The serial position effect of free recall. *Journal of Experimental Psychology,* 64(5), 482–488. https://doi.org/10.1037/h0045106

National Literacy Trust. (2018). *Improving Oracy and Classroom Talk.* https://literacytrust.org.uk

National Research Council. (2000). *How People Learn: Brain, Mind, Experience, and School.* Washington, DC: National Academy Press.

Paivio, A. (1971). *Imagery and Verbal Processes.* New York: Holt, Rinehart & Winston.

Piaget, J. (1952). *The Origins of Intelligence in Children* (M. Cook, Trans.). New York: International Universities Press.

Roediger, H. L., & Karpicke, J. D. (2006). Test-enhanced learning: Taking memory tests improves long-term retention. *Psychological Science,* 17(3), 249–255. https://doi.org/10.1111/j.1467-9280.2006.01693.x

Sedova, K., & Sedlacek, M. (2023). How vocal and silent forms of participation in combination relate to student achievement. *Instructional Science,* 51(2), 343–361.

Snow, C. E. (2010). Academic language and the challenge of reading for learning about science. *Science,* 328(5977), 450–452. https://doi.org/10.1126/science.1182597

Sullivan, N., Heaton, K., & Lowde, L. (2025). *Unlocking Oracy: Enhancing Student Learning and Personal Development.* London: Routledge.

Sweller, J. (1988). Cognitive load during problem solving: Effects on learning. *Cognitive Science,* 12(2), 257–285. https://doi.org/10.1016/0364-0213(88)90023-7

Tomsett, J. (2023). This much I know about … Dylan Wiliam's concept of the NEED/NEAT to know. https://www.johntomsett.com/this-much-i-know-about-dylan-wiliams-concept-of-the-need-neat-to-know/

Waitoller, F. R., & Kozleski, E. B. (2013). Working in inclusive education: Key issues and debates. In T. Loreman, J. Deppeler, & D. Harvey (Eds.), *Inclusive Education: Supporting Diversity in the Classroom* (pp. 25–43). London: Routledge.

Wiliam, D. (2011). *Embedded Formative Assessment.* Bloomington, IN: Solution Tree Press.

Wiliam, D. (2022). Making the curriculum manageable. Interviewed by Mary Myatt and John Tomsett for the Huh Leaders Course.

Willingham, D. T. (2009). *Why Don't Students Like School?* San Francisco, CA: Jossey-Bass.

Wilson, R. A., & Clark, A. (2009). The extended mind in action. In P. Robbins & M. Aydede (Eds.), *The Cambridge handbook of situated cognition* (pp. 55–77). Cambridge: Cambridge University Press.

Wooten, J. O., & Cuevas, J. A. (2024). The effects of dual coding theory on social studies vocabulary and comprehension in elementary education. *International Journal on Social and Education Sciences*, 6(4), 673–691.

3 Behaviour and Attitudes

3.1 What You See and What Lies Beneath

In Chapter 2, I defined learning as a process resulting from experience that leads to a change in knowledge, skills, attitudes or behaviours, changes that may be temporary or permanent. That chapter focused primarily on the first part of that definition: How we help students acquire and develop knowledge and skills through effective teaching strategies.

If all went according to plan, you finished that chapter with a growing toolkit of approaches you were keen to try in your classroom. But knowledge and skills, important as they are, tell only half the story. Two students can experience the same lesson, with the same teacher and the same content, and yet leave with very different outcomes. The difference often lies not in what was taught, but in how students approached the learning itself.

This chapter turns our attention to the other half of the definition – students' attitudes and behaviours. These are the often-invisible forces that shape how students engage with learning opportunities, how they respond to challenge and how they behave when structures are less secure.

By *attitudes*, I mean the internal dispositions, beliefs and emotional responses students bring into a lesson. These might include their level of respect for the teacher, their belief about whether the lesson 'counts', their motivation or their emotional state, ranging from curiosity and excitement to anxiety or indifference. For example, a student may see a lesson taught by a temporary teacher as unimportant, or view it as a chance to relax rather than a continuation of serious learning.

Behaviours, on the other hand, are the outward actions we can see: whether students follow instructions, stay on task, test boundaries, participate actively or disengage. These behaviours are often what teachers notice first, but they are usually driven by what is happening beneath the surface.

Although attitudes and behaviours are closely linked, they are not identical. A student may hold a negative attitude towards a cover lesson, yet behave well due to strong routines or school culture. Equally, a student may respect a teacher

DOI: 10.4324/9781003780410-4

and value learning but still appear disengaged if the task is unclear, too easy or too demanding.

To understand what is really happening in a classroom, particularly when learning falters, we need to consider the context and look beyond behaviour alone. Attitudes shape behaviours and behaviours reinforce attitudes, and both influence whether learning actually takes place.

Figure 3.1 illustrates how students' attitudes towards learning and temporary teachers interact with their behaviours, and how different combinations of the two may present in the classroom. While behaviour is often the most visible aspect of what teachers experience, the table highlights the importance of considering what may be driving that behaviour beneath the surface. Similar outward actions can stem from very different underlying attitudes, and without recognising this distinction, responses risk addressing symptoms rather than causes.

When writing this book, I went back and forth on whether to begin with teacher techniques to improve learning, or with strategies aimed at shaping students' behaviour and attitudes. I ultimately chose to start with learning, because in classrooms where students hold a generally positive attitude towards learning, many behaviour issues can be addressed indirectly through strong instructional design. Research on effective teaching consistently shows that clarity, structure, and appropriate challenge play a central role in reducing disengagement and low-level disruption (Rosenshine, 2012).

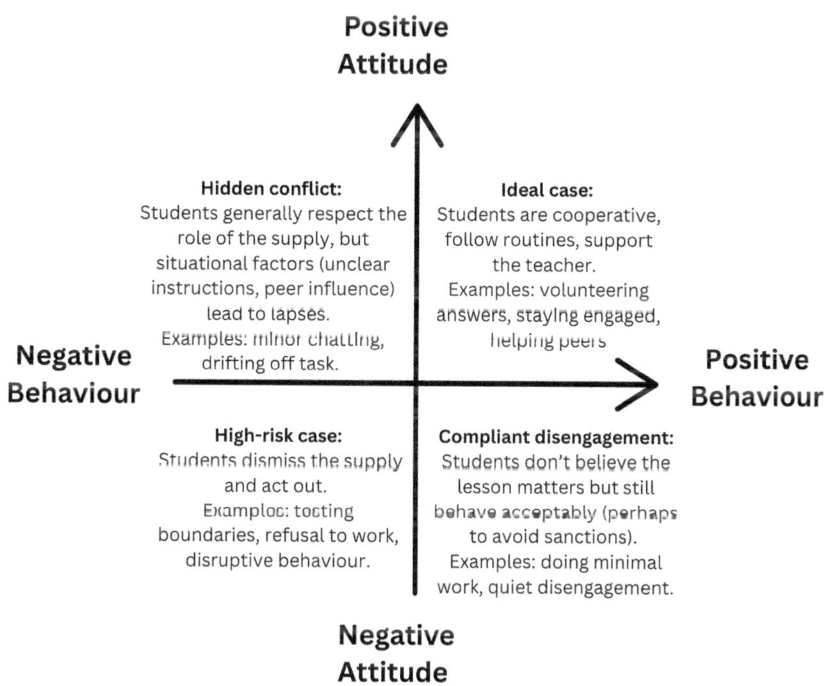

Figure 3.1 Relationship between attitudes and behaviour.

Minor off-task behaviours, such as drifting attention or low-level chatting, are often less a product of poor attitude and more a response to lessons that lack structure, clarity, or an appropriate level of challenge. Kounin's (1970) work on classroom management demonstrated that low-level disruption increases when lessons lose momentum or direction, even among otherwise compliant students.

Creating an environment that closely resembles a normal lesson, even when taught by a temporary teacher, can therefore significantly reduce these issues. Leaving students to work independently for 40 minutes without guidance is likely to lead even highly motivated learners off task. In contrast, breaking tasks into manageable chunks, providing interim checkpoints and maintaining visible teacher presence helps sustain focus and momentum, a pattern consistent with findings on lesson pacing and teacher clarity (Hattie, 2009).

Similarly, when work is too challenging for some students, disengagement often follows. Research informed by cognitive load theory suggests that when tasks place excessive demands on working memory, attention falters and avoidance behaviours are more likely to emerge (Sweller, 1988). The strategies outlined in the previous chapter, such as scaffolding tasks, pre-teaching key vocabulary and providing opportunities to practise retrieval, can prevent this by ensuring that students are able to access the learning without becoming overwhelmed.

In classrooms where students are broadly engaged, where the work meets the needs of most learners and where the temporary teacher actively supports learning, strategies to maintain focus will closely resemble those used by the students' regular teacher. In these contexts, behaviour management becomes less about control and more about continuity, preserving the routines, expectations and learning habits that students already recognise.

3.2 Managing Low-Level Disruption

If you are fortunate as a temporary teacher, you will arrive at a school where students already hold a generally positive attitude towards their learning. That attitude is unlikely to be significantly altered by your presence alone. This does not mean, however, that lessons will be free from behavioural issues. After all, students are still children.

I have lost count of the number of times trainee teachers have observed my lessons and expressed surprise at how well the students behave. Yet when those same trainees step in front of the class themselves, the behaviour often begins to unravel – gradually at first, then more noticeably.

For an observer, it can be difficult to identify what the teacher is actually doing to maintain an environment where behaviour supports learning. The focus is usually on how students are responding, rather than on the subtle, often invisible actions the teacher is taking to guide that response. In this section, I outline a range of strategies that can minimise behaviours that are unhelpful for learning and encourage those that allow the classroom to run more smoothly.

There are many case studies in this book from temporary teachers as well as from educators who are experts in their fields. The next case study is my own. I have chosen to include it here because it highlights something fundamental to managing low-level disruption – the importance of first impressions.

Much has already been written about entry routines, and many schools have clear systems in place. One reason for this is to reduce cognitive load. When students know exactly what to do as they enter a classroom, that is one less decision for them to make, freeing up their attention for learning. Entry routines also provide an early opportunity to identify students who may not yet be ready to learn and who might need additional support.

For me, however, there is an even more important reason to prioritise how I greet students at the door. In *Running the Room*, Tom Bennett (2020) describes the ideal teacher as 'Mary Poppins'. If we take her as a benchmark, it is hard to imagine Mary Poppins beginning any interaction with a child without creating a positive emotional experience. Greeting students, then, is more than a practical routine; it is an opportunity.

That first moment should put a smile on a student's face, communicate that you care and remind them that stepping into your classroom represents a fresh start. As a temporary teacher, you cannot always be certain of a school's specific rules and routines, at least not in enough detail to replicate them perfectly. What you can do, every time, is ensure that the first interaction is a positive one.

The Doorway to Learning: Setting Tone from the Start – Richard Wheadon

I start every cover lesson at the door. Greeting students as they entered allows me to set the tone from the very first second. I want to make it clear that lessons would be calm, structured and purposeful, and I want students to know exactly what is expected. From the moment they entered, I use positive narration: 'Well done, front row – all of you have your books out and are ready to learn'. Highlighting compliance immediately encouraged others to follow the expected behaviour.

Between lessons, during lesson changeover, I took the opportunity to read through the lesson plans and write the key entry instructions on the board. These instructions typically included:

1. Enter quietly.
2. Sit in your seating plan.
3. Take out your book and pen.

If there was no simple task ready for entry, I would use this point to set a brief retrieval activity; for example, 'Write down three things you remember from the last lesson'. This immediately focuses attention and reinforces prior learning.

Once all students are in and engaged with the first task, I circulate the room, continuing to praise those who were meeting expectations. I would try to identify a student showing exemplary effort, say their name aloud and let the whole class know that I would be passing on their name and effort to their teacher in my notes at the end of the day. This not only set a high bar for behaviour and effort but also makes students aware that their positive actions were being noticed and recorded, reinforcing accountability and motivation.

I then pay careful attention to taking the register. This is my first opportunity to show the students that I am not a novice and that I know what I am doing. There is a high probability that at least one student has tried to sneak out of their seating plan. Assuming I have a copy of the seating plan, I would double-check where each student is sitting while calling their names. If I find a student in the wrong place, I give a calm, neutral instruction – 'Please move to your correct seat, thank you' – and then move on quickly without making a big deal of the situation.

All my lessons start the same way. This consistency reduces my own cognitive load and lowers the chances of becoming overwhelmed when something unexpected happens. Your start does not have to look exactly the same, but I encourage you to reflect on mine and write out your own set of instructions. You may even want to take it with you and place it on your desk for the first few lessons. The beauty of supply teaching is that every day is a fresh start, so keep trying out different starts until you find one that you are comfortable with and that achieves the desired outcomes most of the time.

Once students are in the classroom seated and the register complete, the next step as a temporary teacher is to be really clear about your expectations and what you want them to do. This might be explaining how you want them to complete the task, or outlining the boundaries for behaviour during the lesson. Clarity at this stage sets the tone and leaves no room for misunderstanding. Marzano, Marzano and Pickering (2003) highlighted that teacher clarity and consistent expectations are central to managing behaviour effectively, arguably more so than personality or charisma. For temporary teachers, who may not have the time to build strong relationships, this is especially important: students respond better when they know exactly what is expected of them, and a calm, structured start helps establish trust and order from the outset.

To unpick this in more detail, take a few minutes to write out a short script: What are your expectations for your class?

Three Golden Rules

1. Do not talk while someone else is talking.
2. Try your best.
3. Ask for help if you are stuck.

I stick to three rules. We have already discussed the negative impact of cognitive overload in the classroom: If your list of expectations is too long, it becomes difficult for students to remember them all. Permanent classroom teachers have the time to model and reinforce desired behaviours over weeks and months. As a temporary teacher, you do not have that luxury, so it is important that your rules are short and simple.

Not only does having three simple rules prevent students from becoming overloaded, but it also keeps the classroom predictable. Ingersoll (1997) argued that when classroom rules and routines are less visible or inconsistently applied, disruption is more likely to follow. The issue is not that students are inherently more difficult, but that ambiguity in expectations creates opportunities for them to test boundaries. Clear, simple rules substitute (no pun intended) for the missing relationship: They reduce anxiety for students who want to comply and limit the opportunities for those who may be tempted to disrupt.

Having three simple rules also allows you to quickly adapt them to closely mirror the rules of the school. In the first chapter, I suggested that among the first things you ask for upon arrival are the school rules and any school values they may have. Below, I have added some of the values from the school I am currently working in as a temporary teacher to my existing rules:

- *Do not talk while someone else is talking* (Embracing a Positive Culture).
- *Try your best* (Fostering Determined Achievers).
- *Ask for help if you are stuck* (Nurturing Resilient Individuals).

Once students have entered the classroom, my interviews with temporary teachers reveal two key moments when low-level disruption tends to occur:

1. When the teacher requires silence to give instructions.
2. When students have been set a task and the noise level rises to the point that it clearly affects the learning environment.

What follows are a range of strategies that temporary teachers can use to minimise low-level disruption during these moments.

3.3 Positive Narration

Using praise to influence behaviour is nothing new. As early as the 1960s, researchers began to show that what teachers choose to notice and verbalise can significantly shape pupils' conduct. Becker, Madsen, Arnold and Thomas (1967) demonstrated that when teachers increased their use of specific praise for appropriate behaviours, levels of on-task behaviour rose and disruptive behaviour decreased, even without changes to sanctions or rules. This aligns closely with Skinner's (1953) work on operant conditioning, which showed that behaviours followed by positive reinforcement are more likely to be repeated; in the classroom, positive narration acts as immediate social reinforcement, strengthening desired routines without interrupting learning. More recently, research within Positive Behavioural Interventions and Supports (PBIS) frameworks has reinforced these findings. Simonsen, Fairbanks, Briesch, Myers, and Sugai (2008) found that classrooms characterised by higher ratios of positive to corrective interactions experienced fewer disruptions, greater pupil engagement and a more positive classroom climate. Together, this body of evidence suggests that positive narration is not a soft option, but a well-established and effective behavioural strategy grounded in decades of research.

In practice, positive narration is simple, explicit and focused on observable behaviours rather than personal traits. Instead of waiting for low-level disruption to emerge, the teacher actively describes the behaviour they want to see: 'I can see most people already have their book open and the date written', or 'This table has started straight away and is working in silence'. These statements do not interrupt learning or invite debate; they merely direct attention towards success. As more pupils recognise which behaviours are being noticed, those behaviours become the norm, reducing the need for correction and allowing the lesson to maintain momentum, even in unfamiliar classes.

3.4 Self-Coaching Through Deliberate Practice

Although I made the decision to introduce teaching techniques first, many temporary teachers may feel they already have a small set of strategies they are comfortable with and may instead want to start with behaviour management, perhaps with something as practical and immediately useful as positive narration. As someone who has led teaching and learning for much of my career, I find it deeply frustrating that temporary teachers are so rarely given the same level of professional development as their permanent colleagues.

In the UK, newly qualified teachers receive two years of structured mentoring before moving into the same support cycle as experienced staff. This exists for a simple reason: teaching is hard, and even after qualification it takes years to master. In the United States, many substitute teachers receive little or no formal training beyond online compliance modules completed before they start. Yet research consistently shows that one of the most effective ways to improve teaching is through instructional coaching.

A landmark meta-analysis of 60 causal studies by Kraft, Blazar and Hogan (2018) found that instructional coaching produces substantial improvements in teachers' instructional practice (an average effect size of approximately 0.49 standard deviations) which exceeds what is typically seen from traditional professional development models and approaches the difference between novice and experienced teachers.

There are various definitions of instructional coaching which can make it unhelpful. However, I will define it as an expert observing a lesson and identifying a single high-leverage teaching move that, if improved, would have a meaningful impact on learning. That strategy is then rehearsed deliberately, in different forms, until it becomes concrete, before the teacher receives feedback a week or two later on how successfully it has been integrated into their practice before moving onto another area of improvement.

Unfortunately, what is arguably the most powerful form of professional development is rarely available to temporary teachers. However, this does not mean you cannot recreate elements of it through careful self-reflection. One of the key principles of instructional coaching is to work on one small thing at a time, so that you do not overload yourself cognitively.

Returning to positive narration: If, after reading Section 3.3, you realise that you rarely use it, or that you use it inconsistently and it fades when you feel stressed or anxious, then this may be the single target to focus on. Resist the temptation to move on to other strategies in this book until this one has become embedded in your everyday practice.

You can use the proforma that follows to help you decide when it is appropriate to start working on a new strategy.

Daily Teaching Reflection: Trying a New Technique

1. *Goal for Today*: What did you want to achieve by using this technique?
2. *What Worked Well*: Describe what went well when using this technique.
3. *Challenges or Difficulties*: What didn't go as planned? Did anything prevent the technique from being fully effective?
4. *Student Engagement and Response*: How did students respond? Were they more engaged, motivated or on task?
5. *Self-Reflection on Your Practice*: How confident did you feel using this technique? Did stress, time pressure or classroom dynamics affect your use?
6. *Next Steps*: What could you do differently next time to improve your use of this technique?
7. *One Small Target for Tomorrow*: Circle one – I will use this technique again tomorrow / I need more practice / I will try a different technique next.

3.5 Building a Sense of Pace

Another important element of maintaining a positive climate for learning is establishing a clear sense of pace. This is critical in cover lessons, where uncertainty and downtime can quickly lead to low-level disruption. Research consistently shows that pupil behaviour deteriorates in unstructured moments, rather than during purposeful activity. Kounin's (1970) work on classroom management highlighted the importance of *momentum* and *smoothness*, demonstrating that lessons which moved purposefully, with clear beginnings and endings to tasks, experienced significantly fewer behaviour problems. In this sense, pace is not about rushing content, but about removing opportunities for distraction.

One effective strategy is the use of a visible timer on the board. Making time explicit reduces ambiguity and supports pupils' self-regulation by externalising expectations. This aligns with principles from cognitive load theory (Sweller, 1988), as pupils are freed from having to constantly monitor time themselves and can instead direct their attention towards the task. Similarly, brief time reminders such as 'You should be moving onto question three now' act as prompts that maintain focus without interrupting learning. These cues can be strengthened further when combined with positive narration; for example, 'I can see several people already on question three and checking their answers carefully'. By pairing pace reminders with narrated success, the teacher reinforces both momentum and expectation while the lesson continues uninterrupted.

Rosenshine's (2012) principles of instruction further emphasise the importance of structuring learning into small, manageable steps. For temporary teachers, chunking tasks into short phases with clear time limits helps sustain attention and reduces drift, particularly in unfamiliar classrooms. These mini-deadlines increase time on task, a factor long associated with improved engagement and behaviour. This is also why it was important to introduce teaching strategies in the previous chapter, as they play a crucial role in enabling temporary teachers to effectively chunk tasks or add meaningful stages to poorly designed cover work. When activities are too short or lack sufficient challenge, pupils often finish early and begin to lose focus. In these moments, rather than resorting to correction, the teacher can reinforce pace with a time reminder and positive narration: 'I'm really impressed with how quickly you've worked through this. Because of that, I want to add something that will help you remember this learning even more'. By extending tasks purposefully and framing additions as recognition of productive effort, the teacher preserves momentum, sustains attention and deepens learning.

Finally, pace is reinforced through efficient transitions. Kounin identified that unclear or slow transitions were a key trigger for off-task behaviour, while clear signals, countdowns and immediate follow-on tasks maintained lesson flow. In supply lessons especially, a brisk, predictable rhythm communicates authority and purpose. Crucially, moments when all pupils are on task create valuable thinking time for the teacher, allowing them to consider the next course of action and prepare it in advance. By planning the next instruction, resource or extension while pupils are working, the teacher can move seamlessly between activities, preventing pauses in which attention drifts. When pupils know what they are doing, how long it will take and what comes next, behaviour is far less likely to fill the gaps.

Before moving on, here is a case study from an excellent classroom practitioner. David Didau is an educational consultant who has written several books on English, his subject, as well as on the wider educational landscape. When I asked

David to contribute to this book, I didn't have a specific idea in mind. As a reader of his popular Substack, I knew his knowledge and expertise were broad. I simply asked him to think about what is the most useful advice he could give to a temporary teacher. A few months later, he messaged me with a single phrase: 'Messy markbooks'. I share this backstory because, like the lack of instructional coaching that temporary teachers often experience, you also miss the opportunity to observe other educators and learn from them.

As you read David's case study, I want you to imagine yourself in his classroom. Try to get a sense of what it might feel like to be in his lessons, and notice how his intentional decisions affect both student engagement and the pace of learning.

Markbook – David Didau

Although I'm not a supply teacher, a fair amount of my teaching life resembles aspects of supply teaching. Through consultancy work I regularly find myself teaching classrooms full of pupils I have never met, whose names I do not know, whose habits and social arrangements are a mystery and whose prior knowledge I have to infer on the fly, all while being expected to teach something worthwhile, and almost always with a row of adults sitting at the back of the room taking notes, and often being filmed.

When lessons taught to unfamiliar students feel unsatisfying, the usual explanation is behaviour, motivation, or the fact that you do not know the class. Clearly, these things matter enormously. But, increasingly, I think the problem is often more prosaic, and therefore more solvable.

The real problem is memory.

Teaching is already cognitively demanding even when you know a class well. When you do not, the load multiplies. You are holding the (probably unfamiliar) content of the lesson in mind, creating a culture, shaping explanations, listening to answers, scanning the room and making decisions about pacing, while also trying to remember who has spoken, who has not, who offered a hesitant 'I don't know' five minutes ago and who you promised you would come back to once the class had heard a better model. Most of us attempt to manage all of this internally, and most of us are far more confident in our mental bookkeeping than the evidence justifies.

Using mini-whiteboards has helped me see students' thinking more clearly, but they don't solve this deeper problem. I can tell who was paying attention, who was guessing and who was attempting to opt out, but I still found myself relying on my own wobbly recall to distribute attention and opportunity. Who has already answered twice? Who has been overlooked? Who needs encouragement rather than challenge? Who deserves praise that might otherwise be forgotten once the lesson moves on? It was only when I began drawing seating plans and writing names down that this fog began to lift.

The most important tool in classroom management is knowing students' names. The only way this is possible with a new class is to use a seating plan. Sometimes these are provided for me, but often they're not. Even when they are, students' names tend to be too small for me to read. So, I always, without fail, start every lesson by making my own seating plan.

This is hardly unremarkable and – I expect – you already do something similar yourself. I sketch the room, ask students their names and write them in place. When a student answers a question, I give them a tick. I put a dot next to students who 'don't know', and a scribbled note of any contributions I want to refer to later. If a student is taken out of the lesson, I cross their name out so I know to stop scanning the room for them like an idiot. And, crucially, I have my 'messy markbook' on a clipboard so that it's easy to use and harder to lose. This is not to create a record for posterity, but to provide myself with a tool to prop up my fragile working memory.

The most noticeable change is in how quickly using my messy markbook creates a culture of attention and participation. When I tell a student that I'll come back to them, I actually do, because the reminder is there in front of me rather than lurking somewhere in the back of my mind competing with everything else. When I say that I want everyone to think, I can see at a glance who has not yet been involved and ensure I pull them into the lesson.

In one recent lesson, a student – let's call them Seth – opted out early on with a weary shrug and an 'I don't know'. I told Seth that it was fine not to know, but that I wanted them to listen carefully to other's answers and that I would call on them after speaking to a couple of other students. I marked them with a dot, took two answers from others, then returned and asked them to repeat what had been said. He managed it. Praise ensued. On the next question, Seth put his hand up (even though I always make a point of telling students to put their hands down). Without the dot, there's a good chance I'd have forgotten Seth. Without the messy markbook, my promise would have dissolved into something I merely thought I had done.

For anyone who regularly teaches unfamiliar classes, this is rocket fuel. You do not have the luxury of accumulated knowledge built up over weeks. You cannot rely on instinct shaped by long acquaintance. You need some way of making your attention deliberate rather than reactive, so that confidence does not become conflated with understanding and quietness does not become mistaken for disengagement. An annotated seating plan makes this possible by slowing your thinking just enough to ensure everyone is participating in your lesson.

This is not marking, data collection or evidence for anyone else's scrutiny. It is a rough record of attention and thinking in a live classroom that allows you to act immediately on what you notice instead of trusting yourself to remember it later.

I would not teach an unfamiliar class without one now, not because it makes me look organised, but because it helps me notice properly, teaches me where my attention really goes, makes it far more likely that I keep my word and convinces students that I mean what I say.

3.6 Non-Verbal Cues

Cornelius-White (2007) highlights the importance of deliberately fostering positive relationships with students, showing that learner-centred behaviours such as warmth, empathy and positive regard are strongly associated with higher student achievement, increased motivation and reduced disruptive behaviour. This underscores that it is always valuable to try to create supportive connections, even when working in temporary teaching roles. Hamre and Pianta (2005) provide insight into how this can be achieved in practice. Even brief, positive interactions, or micro-gestures, such as greeting students by name, acknowledging effort or offering encouragement, can improve classroom climate, boost engagement and decrease disruptions.

Micro-gestures are small, often subtle actions that can have a powerful impact on relationships in the classroom. Smiles, particularly genuine Duchenne smiles that engage the eyes, signal warmth and friendliness, release oxytocin and foster a sense of connection over time. Gestures such as open palms, uncrossed arms, mirroring a student's posture and offering encouraging nods communicate attentiveness and empathy without words, reinforcing engagement and rapport. Eye contact, even brief but meaningful, shows presence and respect, helping students feel seen. Micro-interactions, such as saying 'Good morning' or noticing effort in work, acknowledge and validate students, meeting their need for recognition. Finally, tone of voice shapes the emotional climate. A warm, calm and friendly tone conveys positivity even when the words themselves are neutral. Together, these micro-gestures create a network of small but cumulative interactions that build trust, engagement and a positive classroom environment.

Six Quick Micro-Relationship Wins for Temporary Teachers

Strategy	Example/Practice	Rationale/Evidence
Greet at the door	A simple 'Morning' or 'Come on in, we'll get started in a moment'.	Signals calm authority and connection. Even short greetings strengthen belonging cues (Roorda et al., 2011).
Learn and use names (even a few)	Glance at the seating plan or ask students to remind you, then use names early in the lesson.	Makes the room feel more personal. Recognition is a powerful motivator (Wentzel, 2002).
Thank the behaviour you want	Swap 'Stop talking!' for 'Thanks to those ready to listen'.	Recognition builds goodwill. Positive framing supports cooperation (EEF, 2019).

(Continued)

Strategy	Example/Practice	Rationale/Evidence
Show presence while circulating	Quietly ask, "How's it going?" or "Do you need a hand?"	Makes students feel seen and supported. Teacher responsiveness predicts higher engagement (Cornelius-White, 2007).
Reset calmly and fairly	'I need everyone's eyes for 20 seconds, then we'll move on'.	A neutral, predictable reset avoids confrontation. Consistency and fairness are linked to improved behaviour (Marzano et al., 2003).
End with appreciation	'Thanks for your focus today; I appreciated that'.	Positive exit notes can shift how students view future supply lessons. Positive closure strengthens classroom climate (Pianta, 1999).

3.7 Active Listening Routines

Active listening routines give temporary teachers a simple, reliable way to gain pupils' attention without raising their voice or relying on authority that has not yet been established. A clear and consistent starting point is a simple countdown cue such as '3, 2, 1 – eyes on me' or '3, 2, 1 – pens down'. This provides pupils with a predictable transition from task to listening and makes expectations explicit. Gestures can be mixed in at this stage, such as raising a hand or pointing to the expected posture, and the teacher can model these behaviours themselves to reinforce the routine. The first time this routine is used, particularly in an unfamiliar class, the teacher may need to pause and wait for full compliance. This moment is where positive narration becomes especially powerful. Rather than repeating the cue, the teacher narrates success: 'I can see most eyes are already this way and pens are down', drawing attention to those meeting the expectation and encouraging others to follow.

Active listening also links closely to the use of choral questioning, introduced in Chapter 2. Rather than viewing listening as passive, choral responses and other active student response strategies invite pupils to participate continuously throughout the lesson, increasing attention and reducing opportunities for drift. Research comparing methods of eliciting responses has found that *choral responding*, where the whole class answers aloud in unison, leads to higher rates of active student responding and improved on-task behaviour compared with traditional individual questioning. This supports greater engagement and behavioural regulation during instruction (Haydon, Marsicano & Scott, 2013).

Used consistently, these routines create smooth transitions into instruction and ensure that listening remains active rather than passive. For temporary teachers, they provide structure, clarity and momentum, three key ingredients for maintaining attention and behaviour in unfamiliar classrooms.

3.8 When It Doesn't Work

Despite having a wide range of strategies to reduce low-level disruption, there will inevitably be occasions when some students' behaviour continues to be challenging. This section is not concerned with the quiet, disengaged students who complete little work but do so without disturbing others; I address strategies for supporting these students in Section 3.9. Instead, the focus here is on behaviour that actively disrupts learning and negatively affects other pupils in the room.

In Chapter 1, I emphasised the importance of familiarising yourself with a school's behaviour policy when starting at a new placement. While preventative strategies should always come first, there are times when these policies must be applied, particularly once other approaches have been exhausted. In such situations, the formal behaviour process may need to be initiated, and in some cases, this can lead to a student being removed from the lesson. For some pupils, a formal warning is sufficient; for others, removal may ultimately be the only viable option to protect the learning of the class.

For a temporary teacher, this can be a difficult and uncomfortable decision to make. The next case study from headteacher Sam Strickland offers reassurance that following this process is both appropriate and supported. I approached Sam for two reasons. First, he has written and spoken extensively about supporting teachers with behaviour, most notably in *The Behaviour Manual: An Educator's Guidebook* (Strickland, 2021). Secondly, I wanted you, the reader, to hear directly from a respected headteacher. Due to the time pressures of school life and the often short-term nature of supply work, it is rare for temporary teachers and headteachers to have the opportunity to meet, let alone discuss behaviour management in depth.

Let this case study provide reassurance that school leaders want temporary teachers to take ownership of the classroom. You are trusted to use the behaviour policy and the range of strategies outlined in this chapter to create the best possible learning environment, even in the challenging circumstances you may find yourself in.

Supporting Supply Teachers with Loud, Distracting Classes – Sam Strickland

A supply teacher walking into a noisy classroom faces a uniquely challenging situation. They are stepping into a room where the routines are unfamiliar to them and potentially not really engrained in the pupils. Equally, the pupils know their classroom environment and the underpinning foundations upon which that particular lesson is built upon better than the back of their hand. The volume of noise as the supply teacher enters the room is high, chatter spreads like wildfire and, despite being polite, pupils are distracting each other and preventing any learning from taking place.

For many supply teachers, this is commonplace. This situation is not a behaviour crisis, but it is an erosion of the learning environment. Unless handled with clarity, consistency and calm authority, it can quickly spill beyond your control.

The following serves as a practical outline of how any given supply teacher can look to handle this all-too-familiar scenario, as follows:

In the First Two Minutes, Set the Tone

The first action requires a brave and strong response to the situation that you are facing with the class. You may feel you are going against the grain of the school's approach here, but upon entering a noisy classroom like this, your first action has to be to set the tone for the lesson ahead. You need to send the class out of the room, line them up single file, insist on absolute silence, establish with the pupils who you are and that as they re-enter the room they are to engage with the work instantly and in silence. Should any pupil look to challenge you here, deal with them instantly. All the time, you need to remember that you are not asking; you are directing. You are establishing the climate for the lesson. Without this in place, the expectations for the rest of the lesson will be built upon sand.

Reset the Room Without Raising Your Voice

Once the lesson resumes, should the noise level begin to be raised, then you need to address this swiftly Loud classes often expect the adult to meet their volume. Do not.

Raising your voice simply adds to the noise.

Instead:

1. Stand still.
2. Wait.
3. Deliver a short, clear instruction in a calm tone: 'I need silence so I can give the instructions. Thank you'.

If you need to do this twice, do it twice. Calm repetition communicates authority far more effectively than volume ever will.

Narrate the Behaviour You Want

In a noisy room, the temptation is to shine a spotlight on the negative:

- 'Stop talking'.
- 'Why are you shouting?'
- 'This is too loud'.

This merely reinforces the behaviour. Instead, narrate the positive:

- 'Thank you to those facing forward'.
- 'I can see table three is ready to begin'.
- 'Most of you are tracking me – excellent'.

Children follow the narrative. Direct their attention towards what right looks like.

Use Seating to Create Calm

You do not need the class teacher's permission to adjust the room in the moment. If you have persistent pockets of noise, simply say:

- 'I'm moving you to help you focus'.
- 'I need you here for now, thank you'.

The message here is clear; the room is a learning space, and you are responsible for maintaining it. Even two or three strategic moves can transform the volume instantly.

Give Short, Structured Tasks to Anchor the Class

A loud room often stems from uncertainty. Without structure, chatter fills the void. Supply teachers should therefore use short, predictable, timed tasks:

- 'You have two minutes to write the title'.
- 'Complete questions 1–3 in silence and you have nine minutes to complete this'.
- 'Pens down, no talking and all eyes on me in 3, 2, 1'.

Timelines create urgency. Structure creates safety. Silence becomes routine rather than a request.

Implement the School's Behaviour System

Try to remember as a supply teacher that you are not a guest who must avoid causing trouble. You are a professional and responsible for safeguarding the learning environment. If pupils continue to be loud or distracting:

1. Issue the school's first step/warning.
2. If behaviour persists, move to the next step.
3. Use on-call or pastoral staff where appropriate.

This is not heavy-handed, nor is it a sign of professional weakness. It is about your being firm and consistent. Consistency is what pupils need most.

Never Get Drawn into Negotiations

Loud classes often try to talk you out of your expectations. Pupils may try to engage you with challenging statements such as:

- 'Our usual teacher lets us sit where we want'.
- 'We always talk during this activity'.
- 'It's not that loud'.

You need to keep in mind that the regular teacher is not in the room today. You are the teacher, and this is about your expectations. Do not debate with children. Instead, a simple, repeatable script is enough:

- 'Today I'm your teacher, and these are the expectations'.
- 'This is what I need from you now, thank you'.

Pass on What You've Seen

At the end of the lesson, record the behaviour of the class and key pupils, both positive and where there are concerns. Supply teachers often feel reluctant to do this, but schools rely on accurate information to support future lessons. A simple note helps key staff to spot patterns and intervene early.

Final Thoughts

A loud class is not a lost class. With calm authority, clear routines and an intelligent use of school systems, supply teachers can reset the climate quickly and effectively.

The key principles are simple:

- Clarity beats charisma.
- Consistency beats confrontation.
- Calm beats volume.

Supply teachers do not need to be superheroes. They just need structures and the confidence to use them.

3.9 Addressing Poor Attitudes

From my own experiences and interviewing temporary teachers, it is clear that in general, students' attitudes toward supply teachers differ from their attitudes toward their normal teacher. A DFE survey showed that 57% of temporary primary teachers and only 35% of temporary secondary teachers felt that they were respected by their students (Department for Education, 2024).

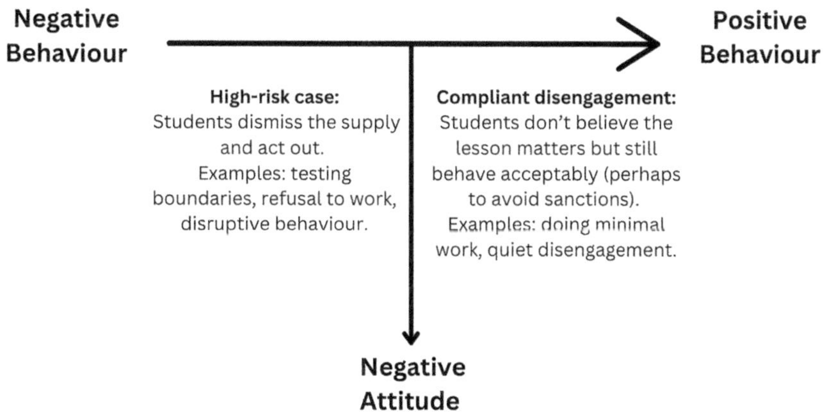

Figure 3.2 The effects of poor attitude.

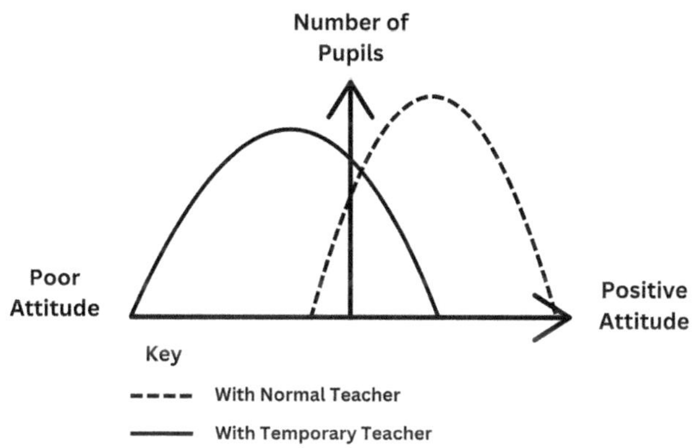

Figure 3.3 How students' attitude shifts with temporary teachers.

Within a school, not all students' attitudes will be uniform. Figure 3.3 is an example of the normal distribution of these attitudes, with some students having a poor attitude, some having excellent attitudes and most sitting somewhere in between.

When a temporary teacher enters the classroom, there is often a noticeable shift in the dynamic and a widening of student attitudes. This can happen for many reasons: the culture of the school, a history of poor cover work being set, negative experiences with previous temporary teachers or even permanent teachers dismissing the work students completed during cover lessons.

The closer you can make your routines and expectations match those of the school, the more likely students are to see you as a teacher, and not just a temporary presence. This applies not only to rules but also to simple routines the school may have. If students are normally expected to stand behind their chairs when they enter a room, incorporate that into your entry routine. If they usually begin with a 'Do Now' task but none has been left for you, create one yourself; have students write down everything they already know about the topic they are about to start.

These small adjustments help maintain consistency, reduce uncertainty and reinforce your authority in the classroom.

Even when you have done everything right, such as establishing routines, setting clear expectations and providing meaningful, purposeful work, there will still be students who work too slowly, show minimal effort or, in the most challenging cases, refuse to engage at all. For some pupils, this may reflect their typical approach to learning. For others, however, it may be situational. The presence of a temporary teacher can prompt students to test boundaries, quietly lower their effort under the assumption that expectations have dropped, or disengage because they struggle with change, lack resilience or need reassurance to re-establish a sense of safety.

Super Communication

For many students, effective communication alone is often enough to improve effort and re-engage them with learning. To understand why, it is helpful to view these moments through the lens of communication.

In *Supercommunicators*, Duhigg (2023) argues that every interaction is made up of what he calls micro-conversations, small exchanges that reveal what a person values, fears or is trying to protect. These moments are where trust is either built or broken. In a classroom, particularly during moments of resistance or withdrawal, these micro-conversations matter more than the task itself.

From this perspective, a student's lack of effort is not simply a behavioural problem or a persuasion challenge. It is a communication moment, a brief human interaction loaded with meaning, assumptions and emotion.

Duhigg outlines several strategies that help people respond more effectively during these moments. Active listening helps individuals feel seen and understood. Asking meaningful, open-ended questions uncovers what is really going on beneath surface behaviour. Mirroring and looping, reflecting back what someone has said and checking for understanding, demonstrates empathy and keeps conversations two-way. Finally, handling difficult conversations involves lowering the emotional temperature rather than escalating it, creating psychological safety rather than resistance.

A student who gives up is almost always communicating something: confusion, embarrassment, low confidence, fear of looking incapable in front of peers or a sense of disconnection from the lesson or the teacher. When we shift our focus from the work itself to the meaning behind the resistance, we begin to operate in exactly the territory Duhigg describes: Connection first, action second.

In other words, before we persuade, we must communicate. Before we communicate, we must understand. And before we understand, we must listen.

This lens does not replace the practical strategies you have already seen. It deepens them. It reminds us that learning is fundamentally relational, and that every small interaction is an opportunity to change the tone, rebuild trust and improve outcomes.

Example

Step 1: Acknowledge and Mirror

Student: 'I don't understand this work. It's too hard'.

Teacher: 'You're finding this really hard right now, and it feels confusing'.

Step 2: Invite Elaboration (Looping)

Student: 'Yes, I don't get what we're supposed to do'.

Teacher: 'Okay, so it's not clear what the question is asking. Which part feels most confusing?'

Step 3: Check Understanding and Guide

Student: 'This step here, I don't know what to do'.

Teacher: 'Ah, you're stuck on this part. Let me explain it a different way and see if that helps. Then you can try it and tell me how it feels'.

Step 4: Confirm and Encourage

Student: 'Oh … I think I see it now'.

Teacher: 'Great. That means you've got this step. Let's take the next one together'.

This works because mirroring shows the student that you are genuinely listening and understanding their feelings. Looping keeps the conversation collaborative, allowing the student to clarify and feel heard. Incremental guidance reduces cognitive overload and gives a sense of progress and mastery. Above all, creating trust and psychological safety lowers anxiety and makes engagement far more likely.

Let's look at another example:

Step 1: Acknowledge and Mirror

Student: 'I hate this subject anyway. It's not important'.

Teacher: 'You're feeling like this subject isn't useful and that it's really frustrating right now?'

Step 2: Invite Elaboration (Looping)

Student: 'Yeah, I'll never need this in real life, it's boring'.

Teacher: 'So you're thinking that what we're doing here won't really matter later. Can you tell me which part feels most boring or useless to you?'

Step 3: Explore Their Perspective and Connect

Student: 'I don't see why we have to learn formulas we'll never use'.

Teacher: 'I get that. It seems like the formulas feel disconnected from anything you care about. Sometimes people find ways this skill connects to things they do or want to do. Can we try looking at it that way together?'

Step 4: Offer Small, Positive Framing

Student: 'I guess maybe it could help if I knew why we use it'. Teacher: 'Exactly. Let's see a real-life example of where this comes up, it might make a bit more sense. Even if you don't love it, understanding it can make the next steps easier, and you'll know it's not wasted effort'.

Step 5: Confirm and Encourage

Student: 'Okay, I'll give it a try'.

Teacher: 'Great. I appreciate you being willing to try. Let's take it step by step together'.

3.10 Work Refusers

In Chapter 2, I outlined several strategies to increase the likelihood that students retain knowledge in their long-term memory. Ultimately, though, no strategy can compensate for a complete absence of effort. If students are unwilling to engage cognitively, to think, attempt and struggle productively, then meaningful learning simply will not take place.

It is important to note that quiet quitters are not your fault as a temporary teacher. As I have mentioned before, students' attitudes toward the lesson have often been set long before you entered the room. That said, this does not mean you should ignore it.

This is another case study from Sam Strickland. I posed this exact scenario to him: What should a teacher do about the 'quiet quitters', students who are compliant, but disengaged? As with the previous case study, his response offers reassurance for temporary teachers. You are the teacher in the room. You should hold high expectations for all students, and when pupils fall short of these expectations, it is appropriate to respond in ways that closely mirror the actions of permanent staff.

The Quiet Refusers: How Supply Teachers Can Respond with Calm, Consistent Authority – Sam Strickland

In every school there exists a particular type of pupil who presents supply staff with a unique challenge. Not the child who is disruptive, nor the one who is loudly oppositional. Instead, it is the quiet refuser. The pupil who sits politely, offers no behavioural issues but simply refuses to work. This behaviour can be deceptively difficult to manage. After all, there is no raised voice, no confrontation, nothing that immediately warrants a sanction. However, the child is not learning, is not engaging with the expectations and valuable classroom time is being eroded. For supply teachers, who are often parachuted into unfamiliar environments without an established relationship, this can feel particularly tricky. I have tried to detail some thoughts and suggestions as to how a supply teacher can deal with this thorny situation, as follows.

Begin with Clarity and Frame This Around Non-Negotiable Expectations

Quiet refusers often thrive on ambiguity. They often exploit the space between 'I would like you to work' and 'This is the expectation in this classroom'. At the start of the lesson, be explicit about your expectations for the lesson ahead. Try to adopt phrases such as 'You are expected to attempt the work set' or 'Everyone is expected to work in silence for the first ten minutes'. Supply teachers need calm clarity when addressing the class. Children crave boundaries, and boundaries create safety.

Use Proximity and Presence Before Escalation

When a pupil quietly opts out, avoid making it a performance. Do not call them out across the room, you risk forcing a fight-or-flight situation. Instead, consider a calm, controlled and measured approach where you do the following:

- Walk over.
- Stand beside the desk.
- Re-state the instruction once, quietly, and state, 'I need you to make a start. I'll check back in three minutes'.
- Then walk away.

This small act of presence communicates that you have noticed, that you care and that expectations still apply, even when behaviour is silent.

Offer Scaffolding and Not Negotiation

A common trap for supply teachers is falling into lengthy debates with pupils about why they should do the work. This only feeds the refusal. A quiet refuser may try to engage you in a negotiation scenario, where they essentially want to barter with you regarding what the expectations in the classroom are. Essentially, they are trying to assert themselves over you. Do not engage in negotiation, and replace this potential vacuum with structure. Make it clear that you want the pupil to make a start by completing the first question or copying out the first sentence and carrying on in their own words or underlining the key terms first. Be explicit, be clear, chunk what you want this pupil to do and be clear about the time frame(s) at hand. This is a supportive approach, but it doesn't relinquish authority. It gives the pupil a foothold and a way to begin.

Use the School's Systems—Because they Exist to Protect You

Supply staff often hesitate to involve and engage with school behaviour and pastoral systems because they 'don't want to cause a fuss'. Those systems, however, are there for a reason: To maintain consistency for pupils and safeguard the adult in the room. If a pupil persistently refuses to meet your expectations, despite clear instructions and opportunities to comply, follow the school's behaviour approach. Often, given how many school behaviour systems operate and function, this is likely to include:

- Noting their name.
- Issuing the appropriate warning or consequence (as per policy).
- Contacting on-call or the pastoral team if refusal continues.

Do not view this as punitive. Instead, adopt the mindset that this is protective. Protective of you and your authority as the adult in the room, and protective of the learning environment as a whole. This also ensures that the message to the pupil is consistent with what they would receive with their usual teacher.

Maintain Professional Detachment

The quiet refuser can sometimes attempt to pull the conversation into the personal. For example, the pupil may try to draw you into a series of combative distraction tactics, such as:

- 'You're not my normal teacher'.
- 'I don't do this work'.
- 'Miss always lets us chat'.
- 'I am allowed to do whatever I want'.

Avoid rising to this, as the pupil is often trying to bait you. Supply teachers must deliberately detach themselves from these emotional hooks. Adopt a simple script that ensures you remain in control and detached. For example:

- 'Today I am your teacher, and the expectation is the same'.
- 'Start your work now, thank you'.

Ensure you deliver such statements with calm finality. It shuts down negotiation and keeps the focus on the task.

Praise Publicly; Correct Privately

When nearby pupils get on with their work, narrate that success:

- 'Thank you, Liam, for getting started straight away'.
- 'I can see this table is working with real focus'.

Positive narration builds momentum. It signals to the refuser that the climate around them is one of productivity and that they are the outlier and not the norm.

Final Thoughts

When faced with a quiet refuser, always log the incident. Pass it on. Share it with the class teacher or pastoral team. This helps the school build an accurate picture of the pupil's learning behaviours. Quiet refusal may not draw attention, but it chips away at learning just the same. For supply teachers, the key is to avoid emotional entanglement and instead lean on clarity, consistency, presence and the school's systems. Remember, though, that you do not need to win a battle. You simply need to uphold expectations with calm authority. For many pupils, that alone is enough to help them re-engage. For the few who persist, the school's structures will support you.

3.11 Unknown Disruptions

Possibly one of the most frustrating scenarios shared with me by temporary teachers is the dreaded anonymous noise. This situation, whether it's a tapping, humming or silly sound whose source cannot be immediately identified is incredibly common and can quickly test a teacher's patience. While it is frustrating, it also provides a valuable opportunity to reflect on and consider the variety of tools suggested in this chapter. Often, it is not a single strategy but a combination of routines, positive narration, attention cues and non-verbal techniques that is required to manage this behaviour effectively.

Scenario: Students make a noise or tap, and the source is unclear.

Step 1: Stay Calm and Neutral

- Keep posture upright, voice firm but calm.
- Avoid immediate confrontation or pointing fingers.

Step 2: Non-Verbal Scanning/Proximity

- Move slowly around the classroom to show awareness.
- Stand near the suspected area; often proximity alone is enough.

Step 3: Positive Narration

- Highlight on-task behaviour: 'I can see most of you are working quietly and getting on with the task'.
- Reinforces expected behaviour without embarrassing anyone.

Step 4: Use Class-Wide Attention Cues

- Countdown: '3, 2, 1 – eyes on me'.
- Gestures: raise hand, fingers up, or model correct posture.
- Keeps the whole class aligned and focused.

Step 5: Concise Anonymous Reminder

- If the noise persists: *"We need the room quiet so everyone can finish their work."*
- Avoid calling out individuals; remain calm and brief.

Step 6: Redirect Attention

- Give a mini-check, choral question, or task checkpoint to engage the class.
- Focus attention on productive work, not the disruption.

Step 7: Ignore if Unknown Source

- If you cannot identify the student causing the noise, do *not* give them further attention.
- Students will eventually lose interest.
- Focus on helping others stay on task and maintain momentum.

3.12 SEND and PP: The Golden Thread

One of the hardest parts of being a temporary teacher is not knowing the students in front of you. You don't have access to EHCPs, behaviour plans, reading ages or pastoral histories. You don't know which students are SEND, which are eligible for Pupil Premium or what any of them might be carrying into your lesson from outside the classroom. That can feel like trying to teach in the dark.

But research offers something reassuring: the things that help SEND and disadvantaged students learn are the same things that help everyone else learn. You don't need special paperwork or inside knowledge to make a difference. You need strong, clear, predictable teaching.

Large-scale research into effective teaching shows that what matters most for closing gaps between advantaged and disadvantaged pupils is the quality of everyday instruction (Hattie, 2009; Education Endowment Foundation, 2018). Similarly, studies of SEND consistently find that learners benefit most from structured, explicit teaching that reduces confusion and cognitive overload (Muijs & Reynolds, 2011; Torgerson et al., 2014).

This is the golden thread:

When teaching is clear, calm, and well-structured, it supports everyone, but it supports SEND and PP students most of all.

For temporary teachers, this is powerful because it focuses on what you *can* control in a single lesson:

- Explaining tasks clearly.
- Breaking work into manageable steps.
- Using examples before asking students to work.
- Keeping routines predictable.
- Reducing unnecessary noise and confusion.

These are not 'SEND strategies' or 'PP strategies'. They are good teaching. But they are also the things that most reduce stress, confusion and disengagement for the students who need stability the most.

When you don't know the individual stories in the room, the best thing you can do is teach in a way that makes learning as accessible and calm as possible. That is how you quietly support SEND students. That is how you quietly close gaps for PP students. And that is why, even on a single day in an unfamiliar school, your teaching still matters.

3.13 Safeguarding

To finish the chapter, I want to shift the focus slightly. I won't go into detail here, as the only statutory training temporary teachers receive is on their role in safeguarding, an area with which you will already be familiar. I share this story for two reasons: first, to demonstrate that, as temporary teachers, you can play a vital role in the safeguarding of students; and second, to highlight a success story of a temporary teacher who started as a cover teacher and discovered their passion working in safeguarding within a school setting.

Seeing the Unseen: A Cover Teacher's Role in Safeguarding – Thomas Michael

If you spend any time in a school, no matter in which capacity, you will no doubt hear the phrase 'Safeguarding is everybody's responsibility'. It could be easy to think that if you are a cover teacher who is working through an agency, and therefore doing a lot of single-day sessions at a variety of different schools, this might not be as applicable to you. Well, you couldn't be more wrong. If you are there for a day, a week, a term or full time – safeguarding is still your responsibility.

The benefit of agency cover staff when it comes to safeguarding is that you are seeing a class with fresh eyes. Sometimes, certain behaviours can become 'the norm' for that student, so they might be overlooked. As a member of staff stepping into that class for the first time, you might observe a behaviour that you feel a little curious about. Make sure that you follow the school's procedures and highlight those concerns. It may well be nothing, but it could be something. Your alert could be the missing piece of a puzzle and could prompt further investigation or support from the pastoral teams, so never second-guess yourself if you feel like you have a concern – put it in, as you never know where it might lead. Also, don't dismiss the possibility of a student making a disclosure to you, either. I know of students that have made disclosures to trainee teachers that had only been with the class for a couple of lessons. Sometimes, young people feel ready to disclose, and if they get a good feeling from someone, they will try and get it out. Don't ever think, 'it won't happen, no one even knows me'.

If you're a cover teacher who isn't working through an agency, then the likelihood is that you are employed directly through a school. This is how I started my career in education; first working on a zero-hours contract, doing days as and when needed, and then working full time. As I was in the school permanently, I ended up seeing practically every student in the school. I would sometimes cover a subject for a term, and eventually I taught A-level psychology for nearly three years as an unqualified teacher. As I was a permanent member of staff, I was allocated additional responsibilities, for example break and lunch duty, and soon built up a lot of positive relationships with students. This actually led to my desire to work in the pastoral side of education, as students would seek me out to talk about things. I had students make disclosures, but I couldn't carry through with the support as that wasn't my role. I moved school, spent two years working as a behaviour support assistant and I am now in my seventh year as a safeguarding and welfare officer/DDSL. Again, this is a factor to consider when taking on a cover role in a school – you will see a lot of the school in a variety of contexts, which gives you a unique insight into some of the students' characters and behaviours.

Regardless of whether you are agency or school based, one of the most important things to do is to make sure you are aware of who the key safeguarding staff are. Make sure that you know what the correct processes and procedures are, should you ever need to use them. Make sure that you keep up to date with safeguarding training and any particular trends. Students may let their guard down in a cover lesson, or they might act out, so you might find work handed in that is covered in doodles. Look at the work, are there any numbers of concern like 14, 18, 88 – known neo-Nazi references, or anything else that could be a concern like references to ideology, mental health, etc. Many things could look innocent on the surface, which is why it is important that you take responsibility for your own knowledge.

I have said it already, but it is well worth repeating: If you have even the slightest concern about a student, pass it on. A DSL would much rather have a number of alerts that amount to nothing, than no alerts at all. Be curious about a student's demeanour and behaviour, and always think about what might be behind that behaviour.

This case study illustrates that, as a temporary teacher, your role in safeguarding is both real and significant. Even brief interactions, fresh observations or small moments of trust can make a meaningful difference in a student's life. While your primary task may be to deliver lessons, your presence in the classroom allows you to notice, question and act when something seems off.

Remember, safeguarding is not about knowing everything or taking on the responsibilities of permanent staff. It is about being alert, aware and proactive. Following the school's procedures, raising concerns and maintaining professional vigilance ensures that every student is supported and protected.

As you take on temporary roles, see them as opportunities to contribute beyond the lesson plan. Each day gives you the chance to strengthen trust, build relationships and play an active part in the wellbeing of young people. Your insights, observations and care matter.

In short: teach with purpose, observe with attention and never underestimate the impact you can have as a temporary teacher in safeguarding.

Conclusion

Managing behaviour and attitudes as a temporary teacher requires clarity, consistency and calm authority. By establishing clear routines, setting simple expectations and using positive narration, you can create a learning environment where students know what is expected and feel supported. Responding to low-level disruption and quiet refusal in a structured and measured way helps maintain engagement and prevents escalation. Building trust through active listening, attention to individual needs and effective use of school systems ensures that all students can participate meaningfully. Ultimately, temporary teachers can have a significant impact on classroom climate, student motivation and learning outcomes, even in short-term placements.

References

Becker, W. C., Madsen, C. H., Arnold, C. R., & Thomas, D. R. (1967). The contingent use of teacher attention and praise in reducing classroom behavior problems. *The Journal of Special Education*, 1(3), 287–307.

Bennett, T. (2020). *Running the Room: The Teacher's Guide to Behaviour*. Woodbridge, UK: John Catt Educational Ltd.

Cornelius-White, J. (2007). Learner-centered teacher–student relationships are effective: A meta-analysis. *Review of Educational Research*, 77(1), 113–143. https://doi.org/10.3102/003465430298563

Department for Education. (2024). *Use of Supply Teachers in Schools: Research Report (RR1449)*. London: Department for Education. https://www.gov.uk/government/publications/use-of-supply-teachers-in-schools

Duhigg, C. (2023). *Supercommunicators: The Science of Connection in the Classroom and Beyond*. New York: Random House.

Education Endowment Foundation. (2018). *EEF Teaching and Learning Toolkit: Closing the Gap*. London: Education Endowment Foundation.

EEF (Education Endowment Foundation). (2019). *Improving Behaviour in Schools: Rapid Evidence Assessment*. London: Education Endowment Foundation.

Hamre, B. K., & Pianta, R. C. (2005). Can instructional and emotional support in the first-grade classroom make a difference for children at risk of school failure? *Child Development*, 76(5), 949–967.

Hattie, J. (2009). *Visible Learning: A Synthesis of Over 800 Meta-Analyses Relating to Achievement*. London: Routledge.

Haydon, T., Marsicano, R., & Scott, T. M. (2013). A comparison of choral and individual responding: A review of the literature. *Preventing School Failure: Alternative Education for Children and Youth*, 57(4), 181–188.

Ingersoll, R. M. (1997). *Teacher Professionalization and Teacher Commitment: A Multilevel Analysis*. Washington, DC: U.S. Department of Education, Office of Educational Research and Improvement.

Kounin, J. S. (1970). *Discipline and Group Management in Classrooms*. New York: Holt, Rinehart & Winston.

Kraft, M. A., Blazar, D., & Hogan, D. (2018). The effect of teacher coaching on instruction and achievement: A meta-analysis of the causal evidence. *Review of Educational Research*, 88(4), 547–588. https://doi.org/10.3102/0034654318759268

Marzano, R. J., Marzano, J. S., & Pickering, D. J. (2003). *Classroom Management that Works: Research-based Strategies for Every Teacher*. Arlington, VA: Association for Supervision and Curriculum Development.

Muijs, D., & Reynolds, D. (2011). *Effective Teaching: Evidence and Practice* (4th ed.). London: Sage.

Pianta, R. C. (1999). *Enhancing Relationships Between Children and Teachers*. Washington, DC: American Psychological Association.

Roorda, D. L., Koomen, H. M. Y., Spilt, J. L., & Oort, F. J. (2011). The influence of affective teacher–student relationships on students' school engagement and achievement: A meta-analytic approach. *Review of Educational Research*, 81(4), 493–529. https://doi.org/10.3102/0034654311421793

Rosenshine, B. (2012). Principles of instruction: Research-based strategies that all teachers should know. *American Educator*, 36(1), 12–19.

Simonsen, B., Fairbanks, S., Briesch, A., Myers, D., & Sugai, G. (2008). Evidence-based practices in classroom management: Considerations for research to practice. *Education and Treatment of Children*, 31(3), 351–380. https://doi.org/10.1353/etc.0.0007

Skinner, B. F. (1953). *Science and Human Behavior*. New York: Macmillan.

Strickland, S. (2021). *The Behaviour Manual: An Educator's Guidebook*. Woodbridge, UK: John Catt Educational.

Sweller, J. (1988). Cognitive load during problem solving: Effects on learning. *Cognitive Science*, 12(2), 257–285. https://doi.org/10.1207/s15516709cog1202_4

Torgerson, D., Torgerson, C. J., Ainsworth, H., Buckley, H., Hewitt, C., & Mitchell, N. (2014). *Improving Writing Quality: Evaluation Report and Executive Summary*. London: University of York/Education Endowment Foundation.

Wentzel, K. R. (2002). Are effective teachers like good parents? Teaching styles and student adjustment in early adolescence. In *Advances in Motivation and Achievement* (Vol. 12). Amsterdam: Elsevier.

4 The Temporary Teacher's Compass: Navigating School and Agency Expectations

4.1 The Hidden Rules of Temporary Teaching

Every temporary teacher I have spoken to has stories of difficult days in challenging schools. But they also have moments that keep them going, moments when everything clicks.

I begin this chapter with one of those moments. It comes from an anonymous post in a Facebook group for temporary teachers. It shows what can happen when all the stars align: When a temporary teacher finds a school that shares their values, where expectations are clear, support is real and they finally feel safe and trusted in their work.

The Power of Supply: Finding Growth and Balance in Temporary Teaching – Anonymous Temporary Teacher

I left my beautiful school four years ago after needing a career break from my 20-year teaching career. I had been a subject lead and truly loved my job. I was terrified about moving onto supply, as I had only worked at two outstanding schools before this, but I signed up with a couple of agencies and took the leap.

At first, I was placed in some challenging schools. But as my agency got to know me, and I got to know myself in this new role, they realised I was reliable, professional and adaptable … all the qualities we already have as teachers, even when we forget!

Over the past five years, I've settled into supply at a handful of local schools. Every year, I've ended up in a long-term placement from Jan to July.

And somehow, I've found myself in a school I have fallen completely in love with – something I never thought would happen again. This time it was a long-term part-time role that I started in January of this year for a maternity cover.

DOI: 10.4324/9781003780410-5

Could I go back to full-time? No. Could I go back to part-time? Absolutely. But with my subject being phased out at my current school, I know I probably won't be returning in a long-term role at the school – and that's okay.

Because here's the heart of what I want to say today: supply is powerful. It's interesting, unpredictable, full of variety, and rich in opportunities to grow. We see so many different ways of working, so many different school cultures. Some we adore; others we're happy to never revisit. But without even realising it, we become incredibly adaptable, resilient people.

Supply shapes us.

With only five weeks left, I'm nervous again about what next year might bring. But I'm also looking forward to the flexibility, to simply covering lessons and then being able to switch off and leave. This year has been intense.

I look at full-time teachers and honestly marvel at how they do it. Teaching is exhausting – mentally, emotionally, physically. It is one of the hardest careers out there.

To anyone else doing supply or thinking about it: there are positives. There is growth. There is balance. And there is hope.

In my interviews with temporary teachers, a clear pattern kept appearing. The happiest, most successful teachers were not those chasing every available booking. They were the ones who had quietly built a small group of schools they trusted, places where they knew the layout, the routines, the staffroom faces and the behaviour systems.

Jim Stewart Allen, a temporary teacher from Washington State since 2014, provides a case study that explains in more detail why this is so important

Inclusion over Isolation: The Power of Relationships for Guest Educators – Jim Stewart Allen

Substitute teaching is a tough job, for many reasons. One of the more difficult aspects of the position is the isolation from not feeling like you have a school that you consistently show up to. This feeling of disconnection towards a school and staff unsurprisingly has a negative impact on the students that substitute teachers teach. Our job collectively as educators is to close this disconnect.

An average day as a substitute teacher can involve some or all of these things; your badge not working while trying to get into the building, getting lost finding the classroom, navigating unfamiliar technology, having to ask the teacher across the hall to help decipher a colleague's cryptic lesson plans, not knowing where the staff bathroom is and countless other obstacles. When piled up, these can make guest teachers feel isolated and alone, and when a substitute teacher is trying to manoeuvre through all these issues, it's tough to concentrate on the actual teaching part, which is the main job they have been hired to do!

The problems just listed obviously hinder the performance of a substitute teacher, but the biggest barrier to being a great guest educator deals with not having the built-in relationships between students or staff that full-time teachers normally get from working consistently in one place. Substitute teaching and consistency normally don't go together, which makes it that much more important to do the work of overcoming this hurdle, and it takes effort from both sides to do this. The school (admin and staff) and the substitute teachers themselves are all responsible. So what can we do, collectively as educators, to not feel isolated from each other?

One of the biggest things a full-time substitute teacher can do is find the schools and classrooms where your style fits best. In my district there are 26 schools, and I've found 4 I work really well in. When I go into those buildings, the office managers are excited to see me, teachers and students know me by name, and I've built a reputation as being a 'good substitute' – one who is respected not just for being likable, but also for ensuring the work gets done. There shouldn't be a day of lost learning just because the full-time teacher is not able to be there. A substitute teacher's primary job is to ensure this happens, and unsurprisingly, a guest teacher who feels isolated and unwelcome will be less able to accomplish this task.

We hear the term 'relationship building' constantly in teaching, and as I mentioned earlier, that's one of the hardest parts of the job. When you're always in different schools, in a different classroom, with different students, relationship building just can't happen as deeply or as quickly. That's why it's so fruitful as a substitute teacher to narrow the number of schools that you work in whenever possible, and to find the administrators and teachers who value having you in their building.

Building a reputation as a 'good substitute', knowing student and staff names, understanding how specific teachers like their classrooms to be run, knowing how specific students learn and tailoring lesson plans to fit their needs are all aspects of relationship building and will help exponentially in making someone a more successful guest teacher. Simply put, when a substitute teacher knows the kids and the staff, and when the kids and staff know the substitute, more effective learning gets done.

As a substitute teacher, you should be building a small-to-medium list of classrooms and schools you work best in, that give you the ability to consistently build relationships with the full-time students and staff. As a classroom teacher and part of a school wide community, you should be building relationships with your substitute teachers to ensure they come back. This will establish that students know who is coming in the next day, so that they feel safe, comfortable and excited to learn.

The opposite of isolation is inclusion, and when we as educators put in the work to connect substitute teachers within the school communities they serve, we can have more effective days of learning.

Stability changes everything. It means you know what time to leave the house. You know where to park. You know who to ask for help when the photocopier jams. And you know what kind of behaviour you are likely to walk into.

In other words, you are no longer gambling every morning.

This chapter shows you how to build that kind of network. Drawing on my experience as a senior leader responsible for staffing, alongside insights from headteachers and supply agencies, I will explain how schools decide who gets booked, who gets rebooked and who quietly disappears from the system.

Whether you are just starting out in supply or trying to move from unstable day-to-day cover into something more secure, this chapter will give you practical tools to reduce your risk in the eyes of schools and increase your chances of being invited back. By the end, you will also see how the skills you develop as a temporary teacher can become powerful evidence when applying for a permanent post, if that is the direction you eventually choose.

Risk

Most temporary teachers believe they are being judged on their teaching. They aren't. They are being judged on something far more basic: Risk.

When a school books a temporary teacher, they make a quiet calculation:

- Will this person turn up?
- Will they keep pupils safe?
- Will they make life easier or harder?

Agencies make the same calculation. Cover managers make the same calculation. Heads of department make the same calculation.

The supply teachers who get called back, the ones who move from day-to-day scraps to steady, long-term work are not necessarily the best teachers in the building. They are the ones who make themselves the lowest-risk option. This chapter is about learning how to do exactly that.

4.2 Working with Agencies

The Department for Education's (DfE) *Use of Supply Teachers in Schools* research shows that most schools prefer to build close working relationships with one or two supply providers, typically local to their area. These preferred partnerships allow schools to work more closely with agencies that understand their context, expectations and routines and, critically, help them reduce the risk involved in bringing temporary teachers into their classrooms (Department for Education, 2024).

As one secondary school leader explained in the DfE study:

> We use two agencies local to the school, one which we've had a very long-term relationship with, and the other a more recent one. But they tend to supply us

> the same people because we are quite choosy about who we work with. We've built up relationships with those organisations so that we have the flexibility to say to them, 'We want X, but not Y'.

In other words, schools are not simply buying cover; they are managing uncertainty by narrowing the field to trusted teachers who have already demonstrated reliability, familiarity with the school's routines and a strong fit with their culture. This view is echoed by one supply agency representative, who noted that most schools prefer to develop partnerships with one or two preferred suppliers that understand the local area and can provide access to a pool of 'tried and tested' supply teachers who are a 'good fit' for their school context.

The role of the agency, therefore, is an important one for temporary teachers. However, it is common for temporary teachers to sign up with several agencies at the same time, due to the fact that some schools will use only one or two agencies, and temporary teachers could be missing out on local schools that could be a perfect match just because that school doesn't work with the agency they are signed up for.

I was fortunate with the agency I signed up with, as I have always had a steady stream of work. I believe much of this was due to the strong relationships my agent had built with a number of local schools over time. The reputation of your agency and the standing of your agent with schools as well as their knowledge of school systems cannot be underestimated. A good agency can do more than help with employment; they can also support temporary teachers with some of the other challenges the role brings, particularly feelings of isolation or not being valued professionally.

When I interviewed temporary teachers about their favourite things regarding their agency, I received many positive responses. For example:

> Taking time to get to know you and remember things about you that add personal touches like wishing me luck on my driving test, makes you feel like a person.

Some agencies go further, offering social events or one-on-one opportunities, like inviting clients for coffee to catch up and see how they're doing:

> Doing simple things like going for a coffee gives a personal touch in such a money-focused industry, and it makes a massive difference.

One story in particular was so moving that I feel it is important to share.

> I can't praise my agency enough. About three years ago, my daughter was hospitalised with a condition called DKA at the age of four. DKA can be fatal, and she was quickly diagnosed with Type 1 diabetes. I was frantic about work and worried about keeping my agency updated. My agent simply told me to stop messaging, stop worrying about work, and get in touch when I was able. I still remember standing outside the hospital, crying, because that human touch meant so much at such a traumatic time.
>
> – Rowan Louisa

I share this story to highlight an important point: As temporary teachers, you deserve this level of respect. Some of you may not be used to it and may have left toxic schools because you felt uncared for. But this story is a reminder that there are agencies and schools that do care about you as an individual.

We all deserve this kind of kindness in our working lives. Just like the story I shared at the start of this chapter, I encourage you not to settle for less. Seek out agencies and schools that treat you with respect and compassion, and build relationships where you feel supported and valued.

Unfortunately, for American temporary teachers reading this chapter, you may feel a little frustrated when reading about the positive relationships between some agencies and their clients. In the United States, it is common for all bookings to take place through an app, which removes the personal aspect of temporary teaching completely. If this is the case for you, it is even more important to make a strong impression when you arrive at a school where you could see yourself working. Many of my American colleagues report that schools often request a specific temporary teacher by name in the future if they were happy with the cover provided.

Due to an excellent working relationship with my agency and the support I had been given, I asked them to share what advice they would give temporary teachers to give the best possible change of success.

Standing Out in Supply: Building a CV and Reputation that Gets You Booked – Paul Matthias, National Director of Education at Hays

Supply teaching offers flexibility, variety and the chance to make a real difference in schools, but it's also a competitive field. Standing out isn't just about having the right qualifications; it's about how you present yourself and respond to the expectations of schools and agencies. With teacher shortages continuing across the UK and demand for supply staff rising, it's important you ensure your CV and approach are working for you.

Supply teaching success starts with a strong CV and application. These documents are your first impression, so they need to showcase adaptability, professionalism, and readiness for the classroom. Schools want clear evidence that you can manage behaviour effectively and adapt quickly to different environments, whether that means confidently leading a secondary class or creating an engaging learning experience for younger pupils. Highlight experiences where you've stepped into unfamiliar settings and maintained control, or where you've adapted lesson plans across key stages. Flexibility is a prized quality in supply teaching, so make sure your CV demonstrates your ability to cover different subjects and year groups. Including a defined section on your availability, days, weeks, even ad-hoc cover, can put you ahead, since schools often need cover at very short notice.

Professional development is another key differentiator. Supply agencies and schools value teachers who invest in their growth, so include any recent CPD courses, especially safeguarding, special educational needs and disabilities (SEND) or phonics training. A sustained commitment to learning reassures employers that you're proactive and reflective in your practice.

Understanding what schools and agencies look for helps you position yourself effectively. Schools tend to prioritise teachers who can build rapport with students quickly, maintain discipline and integrate smoothly into their policies and culture. They want professionals who arrive prepared, punctual and positive – as well as being reliable.

For agencies – as well as a good track record – they are looking for teachers who confirm bookings promptly, turn up on time and deliver consistently. Honesty about your experience and availability builds trust and strengthens your relationship with recruiters.

Current recruitment trends underline why it's so important to stand out. According to the *Hays UK Salary and Recruiting Trends 2026* guide (Hays, 2025), skills shortages remain extremely high, with 96% of employers reporting gaps and 79% predicting a shortage of suitable applicants in the year ahead. For supply teachers, this creates an opportunity to secure rewarding roles, provided you present yourself as dependable, adaptable and skilled.

When it comes to pay, supply teaching can offer competitive rates that reflect your experience and flexibility. Qualified teachers typically earn more than unqualified staff, and those who take on senior responsibilities or specialise in areas like SEND often command the highest rates. Working in London usually means a higher salary compared to other regions, and long-term placements often pay more than short-term cover. If you're looking to maximise your earnings, consider building expertise in high-demand areas such as special educational needs or STEM subjects, as schools value these skills and are willing to pay a premium for them.

Reliability is often the deciding factor in repeat bookings. Schools frequently require cover at very short notice, and teachers who confirm quickly and perform well are the ones agencies call again. Subject specialisms can also give you an edge – there's increasing demand for teachers with expertise in areas such as STEM subjects, SEND and modern foreign languages. These roles are widely recognised as shortage areas in UK education according to the *Teacher Labour Market in England Annual Report* (Worth & Faulkner-Ellis, 2024).

SEND specialists play a vital role in supporting pupils with additional needs, such as autism, ADHD or speech and language difficulties, by adapting lessons and ensuring inclusive learning. If you have skills in any of these areas, make sure they are clearly highlighted in your application, as schools and agencies place a premium on flexibility and specialist knowledge.

Safeguarding is essential – and all schools expect supply teachers to have a thorough understanding of child protection policies and to hold a current DBS check. It's recommended that you sign up for the DBS Update Service so you can stay informed.

Demonstrating your knowledge and readiness in these areas reassures both schools and agencies that you can create a safe, compliant learning environment from day one.

Supply teaching is more than just filling a gap; it's about making a positive impact in every classroom you enter. By tailoring your CV, demonstrating flexibility and understanding what schools and agencies value most, you can position yourself as a trusted professional in a sector that needs your skills. With demand high and salaries rising, now is the time to take control of your supply teaching journey and ensure you're ready to navigate the opportunities ahead.

4.3 What Research and Practice Tell Us About a Strong Supply Teacher CV

Research echoes the advice of Paul Matthias: If schools and agencies are making decisions based on perceived risk and trustworthiness, your CV is one of the first and most important opportunities to signal that you are low risk and high value. The evidence from recruitment research, job-market studies and advice from school leaders consistently highlights several features that distinguish strong supply teacher CVs from weak ones.

1. Clarity, Brevity and Readability

   Recruitment research shows that hiring professionals spend very little time on a first scan of an application – often as little as 6–10 seconds per CV (TheLadders Eye-Tracking Study, 2012).

   For this reason, a good CV is:

   - Clear and easy to skim.
   - Well-structured with headings.
   - Free of unnecessary detail or dense blocks of text.

   This matters for supply teaching especially, because agencies and schools typically review many applications quickly and need to form a reliable impression within moments.

   Practical tips:

   - Use clean headings (e.g., 'Professional Profile', 'Teaching Experience', 'Key Achievements', 'Professional Skills', 'Qualifications').
   - Keep each role description to 3–6 bullet points maximum.
   - Avoid long paragraphs.

2. A Strong Professional Profile

   A professional profile, sometimes called a personal statement, sits at the very top of a CV and gives a brief snapshot of who you are, what you bring to the role and why you are a strong fit. Career guidance sources highlight that recruiters often spend only a few seconds on their initial scan of an application, so a clear, tailored profile can help them quickly grasp your value and encourage them to read on. Many employers report that when they are short on time, a strong personal profile helps them understand at a glance why a candidate is relevant for the role, particularly in competitive job markets where first impressions count (Prospects, 2025).

   Who are you?

   What *value* do you bring especially to temporary contexts?

   For temporary teachers, this profile is an opportunity to highlight your:

   - Flexibility
   - Classroom management strengths
   - Ability to adapt to varied contexts
   - Track record of reliability

Example Snippet

Secondary Science teacher with five years' experience across multiple school settings. Strong behaviour management, flexible planning and a proven record of applying cognitive science in the classroom to enhance learning. Reliable, punctual and committed to supporting learning continuity.

This kind of profile immediately signals what schools care about.

3. Evidence of *Concrete* Impact

   Recruitment research and employer guidance emphasise that specific, measurable examples on a CV are far more effective than vague or generic statements, as they allow hiring managers to assess a candidate's actual contribution and potential value (SwiftScout, 2025).

   For temporary teachers, this means:

   - Demonstrating what you *did*, not just what you can *do*.
   - Using numbers/metrics where possible.
   - Briefly pointing to outcomes.

Example Bullets

These kinds of specifics reassure schools and agencies that you can handle varied contexts.

- Consistently implemented school behaviour policy by applying positive and negative reinforcement in line with expectations.
- Adapted cover lessons to support learning by embedding retrieval practice and reducing cognitive load through pre-teaching key vocabulary.

4. Evidence of Versatility Without Chaos

   A common CV pitfall for supply teachers is an overly long list of short stints that looks chaotic rather than versatile. To avoid this:

   - Group similar roles where appropriate.
   - Emphasise *responsibilities and outcomes* rather than just dates.

Example

Supply Teacher (Various Schools) – 2021–Present

- Delivered high-quality cover lessons in English, Maths, and Science across 12+ schools.
- Consistently praised for behaviour management and adaptability.

   This format shows breadth without diluting professionalism.

5. Professional Presentation and Error-Free Writing

   Recruitment studies show that spelling and formatting errors on CVs significantly reduce recruiters' perceptions of a candidate's competence and interview chances, even when experience is strong. This is especially relevant in teaching, where written communication is central to the role (Sterkens et al., 2023).

   Before submitting:

   Spell-check.

   Consistent formatting (dates, fonts).

   One clear PDF, not multiple versions.

4.4 School Leadership

One thing I wanted to bring to this book was the voices of practising headteachers, to help start closing the gulf between them and the temporary teachers in their schools. I asked headteachers what advice they would give to temporary teachers if they had the chance to sit down with them. Here is the perspective of Sam Crome, Primary Headteacher and author of *Power of Teams*: (Crome, 2023):

Supply Teaching Insights: Five Strategies from a Headteacher's Perspective – Sam Crome

Over the course of my career, leading both secondary and primary schools, I have had a mixed relationship with supply. For many years, I felt so strongly about the high rates that get applied to a day's work that I was adamant not to use agencies at all. But over time my view has changed, and, particularly having been a headteacher in a one-form entry primary school, I do understand that there can be a lot of value in supply agencies and staff.

In the last few years, I have worked with some brilliant teachers who actively choose to work in supply, enjoying the flexibility it provides and the wide range of experiences that they get from working in so many schools. I salute your choice; the lack of familiarity and predictability in your week is difficult, and without your support, schools couldn't function properly.

Based on my experiences, here are five tips I would give to supply teachers who are looking to excel in their role:

1. *Get to know the school:* If you can, try to get to grips with the ethos and culture of the school. Every school has a very different climate when it comes to behaviour, relationships, rewards and sanctions. Ask as many questions as you can about different scenarios, and try to understand 'how we do things here' – the school team will be pleased that you have!
2. *Policies are there to be followed – don't shy away from them*: I've met many teachers who hesitate to enforce the behaviour or uniform policy because of how they might be perceived, with the common worry that applying a sanction may make them look less competent. But school policies and procedures work properly only when they are applied consistently by staff. It creates clarity for children and adults, and it means everyone gets a fair, predictable experience. The SLT who has asked you to come in and teach for the day will be delighted for you to uphold the same expectations and routines as their usual staff, so do not be afraid to use 'on call', set a detention or follow one of the uniform routines.
3. *When in doubt, just ask*: Supply teachers often say to me that they don't want to be a bother or to take up anyone's time during the day. I really enjoy working with curious, conscientious staff, whether they are part of our regular team or come in externally; questions spark conversations and evaluation and ultimately lead to clarity. On many occasions, supply teachers have asked me something during the day that I've forgotten to impart, and I have been so glad – their question led to something being done better, which ultimately means the children got a better experience!

4. *Invest in your professional learning, and ask the school about theirs*: I recently had an amazing discussion with a supply teacher about an education book we had read, and it lead me to ask them how they kept up with professional learning while not being anchored in a school with a dedicated PD offer. It turns out we were in the middle of reviewing our feedback policy at the same time that this supply teacher was doing some reading around live modelling and live marking, which meant that we had a meaningful conversation and learnt from each other. The point I'm trying to make is that some education leaders won't assume that you are a teacher who is looking to grow and improve, so try starting a conversation about this with school staff and see what you can learn both ways.
5. *Give the school feedback*: Every education leader is a bit different, but I certainly want to know what the reality is when it comes to the experience a supply teacher gets when they come in for a day's work. I want to know how easy or hard it was to get set up and logged in. What was it like finding the resources? Was the work good enough, or long enough? Did our processes help or hinder your teaching? How did the children respond to you? The best education leaders care about this and will use your feedback productively.

Having led staff recruitment at a large secondary school, I can echo Sam's views. Two particular examples spring to mind. First, the discussion with a temporary teacher about professional development. A few years ago, when recruiting for a science teacher, a candidate asked to meet me to get a feel for the school and its culture. Normally, we offer this only for senior roles, but since she had taken the effort to contact the school, I put some time aside for the meeting. We had a wonderful chat about all things teaching and learning, and as she left, I hoped she would submit an application.

These informal conversations can shape the views of those in schools who make recruitment decisions. If you find the opportunity, don't shy away from it. Many temporary teachers have shared with me that senior leaders often appear uninterested, but schools where leaders are disengaged are not the ones you want to invest your time and energy in anyway.

When you find a school you like, and a friendly face among the leadership team, don't miss the chance to share your expertise. You never know when they might need someone with your skillset, and conversations like the one Sam had can ensure your name is top of mind when they contact the supply agency.

Some temporary teachers may not know what to say in these situations. Hopefully, the examples in this book will help you strike common ground. For instance, you might tell a headteacher how much you appreciated the cover work that was set, noting that the text already had key vocabulary underlined, which made it easier for you to pre-teach important terms and then set up paired talk to get students to think carefully about these words in a variety of contexts to make them more concrete. You could also discuss how a retrieval quiz at the start of a cover lesson helped students settle calmly and how implementing it consistently could benefit temporary teachers.

The second key idea to take from Sam's case study is the danger of lowering expectations in your classroom. When students challenge your authority or do not engage with the work set, it can be tempting to lower your expectations, let things slide or avoid using the policies you have been provided with. This is not a criticism of temporary teachers; it is an issue seen across all classrooms. I have observed it in schools up and down the country in my role as an independent consultant.

There is, however, an added challenge for temporary teachers. As Sam notes, using the school's systems such as removing students from the classroom can feel as though you might appear less competent to the permanent staff. But as Sam reassures, 'The SLT who has asked you to come in and teach for the day will be delighted for you to uphold the same expectations and routines as their usual staff'.

It can be all too easy in any classroom to operate by an unwritten rule: As long as everyone keeps quiet, we won't have any problems. After all, it is much harder to challenge a student who is doing nothing than to let it pass. As a temporary teacher, maintaining high expectations in the face of such challenges can be particularly difficult, when you walk past and smile at a headteacher who ignores you, when you seek clarification from a colleague who is too busy to help or when you encounter cover work that has been rushed together in a couple of minutes.

It is easy in these moments to think, 'Well, it's not my fault the students are like this', and in many ways, you would be correct. A school with a poor culture can make teaching more challenging, but it should never be a reason to lower your personal expectations. As motivational author Ralph Marston (1998) famously says, 'Don't lower your expectations to meet your performance. Raise your level of performance to meet your expectations'. Maintaining your own high standards ensures that your teaching remains consistent and professional, even in difficult environments, and models resilience and accountability for students.

Beyond the impact on students, maintaining high expectations and valuing your professionalism has important benefits for you as a temporary teacher. Research shows that educators who maintain a strong sense of professional identity, including confidence in their role and a commitment to high-quality practice, tend to experience higher levels of job satisfaction, wellbeing and engagement. When teachers feel confident in their skills and committed to their work, they derive more meaning and fulfilment from their practice, which supports both their performance and their emotional resilience (Sun et al., 2022). By upholding professional standards consistently, even in challenging or unfamiliar classrooms, temporary teachers not only enhance learning outcomes for their students but also strengthen their own sense of purpose and professional growth.

4.5 Permanent Work

As previously stated, around 47% of temporary teachers in the UK intend to secure permanent posts. This can be challenging for a number of reasons. First, there is the issue of the finder's fee. If a school where you are already working on a temporary contract advertises a permanent role, the agency can collect a substantial fee often worth thousands of pounds if you are successful in securing the position. The same can happen if they put your name forward for other posts. With this in mind, it is important that if you see a job advertised, you submit your own application rather than relying on an agency to do it on your behalf. (Department for Education, 2024).

Secondly, having a CV or application filled with short-term placements can unfortunately create a bias in the minds of those hiring, suggesting that you may not be ready for a permanent position. I know this from personal experience as a hirer; it was easy to assume that if a candidate had been exceptional, they would already have been snapped up. While you cannot completely remove the stigma attached to long-term supply work, this book aims to provide you with the tools to demonstrate to prospective employers that you not only have the qualities to help their school thrive, but also that the unique set of skills and experience you have developed over time will allow you to add real value to their school.

As discussed previously, we can increase the chances of moving knowledge into our long-term memory by revisiting it. For those considering permanent work, now is a good opportunity to reflect on some of the key ideas in this book – focused on teaching, learning, behaviours and attitudes – and revisit them. Take a look at a cover letter you have written in the past and consider what you would want it to look like in six months if you started to embed some of the ideas from this book.

For example, a generic statement such as:

> In my role as a temporary teacher, I have tried to build positive relationships with students and create opportunities for them to learn.

could be enhanced to something like:

> In my role as a temporary teacher, I have demonstrated flexibility and calmness under pressure by successfully implementing school behaviour systems across a variety of settings to uphold the high expectations and values of each school I work in. I have enhanced learning by adapting lesson plans to include opportunities for retrieval practice, reducing cognitive load by pre-teaching key vocabulary, and creating chances for students to think more deeply, increasing the likelihood that knowledge is transferred to their long-term memory.

Regardless of whether you are looking for a permanent role or not, writing a new cover letter based on the principles in this book can serve as a tool to support your vision of professional growth over the coming months. Changing daily habits is challenging for many reasons, which we will explore in the next chapter. However, this cover letter can act as a catalyst for that change, helping you clarify your goals and the steps you want to take to achieve them.

I end this chapter with another case study from a headteacher. Chris Passey, co-author of the book *Succeeding as a Deputy Head: The Ultimate Guide to Deputy Headship* (Kohlbeck & Passey, 2026) and host of the podcast *EduPulse*, generously shared his thoughts on how to support temporary teachers. Init ially, Chris told me he had never given it much thought. However, after writing down his ideas, he admitted that he hadn't realized he had so many opinions about temporary teachers.

My hope is that this book, in addition to supporting its intended audience of temporary teachers, will also help spark conversations within schools about the role we all have to play in ensuring temporary teachers can succeed.

The Perfect Supply Teacher – Chris Passey, FCCT, Headteacher of Kimichi School, Birmingham, UK

When considering the desirable attributes of a supply teacher, I think we first must address the chasm of difference between the job title and how they are treated and perceived in our schools. Long-standing images of 'cover' teachers not being able to control classes sit in our collective psyche and are always the trite choice of film directors when wishing to display chaos and disorder in the classroom.

Amongst the many arguments about the current teacher recruitment crisis, I think we are struggling to recognise that ECTs have 'teacher' in their title, which means – at least in this example – that they are qualified practitioners and should be treated as such; they seldom are. Instead, they are taken under the wing of hastily appointed heads of teaching and learning, foisted into an ill thought-out and embryonic coaching programme and treated as though they have no experience of the job into which they are diving head-first. Of course, we know the real experience is in the field, out there in our classrooms; but that doesn't detract from the fact that they are not treated as teachers, however early they may be in their careers.

I find that this attitude is even more pervasive when it comes to supply teachers. When was the last time you heard their full title being used?

'Lilly, have we got supply in today', 'Mark, call the supply agency' – the word 'supply' has become a pejorative term, and one that suggests a production line of adults to work through until the right one is found. Supply teachers are a quick fix to a permanent problem, but we rarely discuss and appreciate the vast contextual adaptations of the job. From primary to secondary settings, myriad subject disciplines and the disabling knowledge of the student body that know they are impermanent and, no matter the culture of respect the school espouses, easily manipulated or taken advantage of.

If the deck is thusly stacked against our supply teacher colleagues, how, then, are they to succeed?

Professional Curiosity

Rarely is there enough time between getting the call at 7:30 a.m. and arriving at the school to research the behaviour policy and pastoral systems, and yet knowing these elements is essential to the supply teacher to glide seamlessly into the school without being too much of an 'other'.

Getting into the school early and investigating basics such as classroom entry routines (these should be easy to spot or explained if the culture of the school is strong enough): A lack of this information should be taken as the opportunity to form your own system.

Being professionally curious is also about seeing the cover you've been given and learning to interpret it through your own teaching lens. Supply teachers are exactly that; if we wanted supply humans who can read instructions, I'm sure we'd come up with a snappier and more honest title. I want supply teachers who bring their own world experience to the lessons, adapting lesson plans and cover so that they can physically teach as much of the content as possible. The best supply staff I have worked with are professionally curious enough to even go slightly off piste, writing notes about what they've covered from the supply notes and commenting on additional thoughts and materials. Here's what I mean:

Supply Note

Read pages 7–11 and make notes, answering the questions on page 12.

Ideal Action

Supply teacher sets the class off on a five-minute do-now, if they've not had chance to read the notes, in which case this becomes the perfect opportunity. Incidentally, every supply teacher should have a plethora of do-now activities that have been successful at academically containing a class and allowing focus.

Once the material has been read by the supply teacher, they guide the class through the note-taking, asking questions, suggesting headings and creating opportunities for contextually appropriate questioning and assessment of understanding – anything from mini-whiteboards to turn and talk.

What the supply teacher has done here will, if done with empathy and understanding of the craft of teaching, engender the class to being more able to engage with the lesson being taught and not a supply person simply reading instructions

Teacher and Human

Supply teachers should come with their own set of rules that can be explicitly taught to each of the classes as soon as they enter the room. As I've said, it's not always possible to know the specific rules that govern good behaviour in a new school, but a good supply teacher knows the basics and can affirm these right from the outset:

> Good morning 9S, my name is [...] and I am your teacher for the next 50 minutes. I've heard a lot of really good things about this school and I'm looking forward to seeing them for myself.
>
> Now, before we start I just wanted to make a few things clear: Please don't talk while I'm talking; when I do speak, please make sure there's nothing in your hands and you are looking at me...

There's an infinite number of ways this opening can be scripted based on the individual beliefs of the teacher, but the basics of common decency and respect for the role of the teacher should be paramount. If you ask and don't tell and give before you take, a supply teacher will be more likely to succeed in this alien environment.

The Rest of Us

Finally, we must look to school leaders to set the culture of supply teachers by providing, without issue:

- A simplified safeguarding process designed for supply teachers.
- A class list with identifiable SEND.
- Behaviour policy headlines.
- Either (a) an easy-to-use MIS (!) or (b) a paper or cloud-based tool that allows swift and uncomplicated communication and recording.

There are so many more things we can be doing in schools to welcome supply teachers and help them succeed in our settings because the system needs to support their sense of professional identity, not disrobe them of it by not treating them as equals but as convenient stop-gaps.

There is no such thing as the perfect supply teacher. But there is an opportunity for schools to become perfect supply teacher homes, and this is what we should be striving towards, so that one can feed and ensure the existence of the other.

Conclusion

Temporary teaching isn't just a stopgap; it's an opportunity to grow, adapt and prove your professionalism. Success comes from managing risk, building relationships and showing reliability. Strong CVs, clear evidence of impact, and attention to school culture make you the teacher whom schools and agencies want to call back.

Respect yourself, respect the students and respect the schools you work in. Do that, and even temporary roles can become meaningful, rewarding and a springboard to long-term opportunities.

References

Crome, S. (2023). *Power of Teams.* Woodbridge, UK: John Catt Educational.

Department for Education. (2024). *Use of Supply Teachers in Schools: Research Report (RR1449).* London: Department for Education. https://www.gov.uk/government/publications/use-of-supply-teachers-in-schools

Hays (2025). *Hays UK salary & recruiting trends 2026.* London: Hays plc.

Kohlbeck, A., & Passey, C. (2026). *Succeeding as a deputy head: The ultimate guide to deputy headship.* London: Bloomsbury Education.

Marston, R. S., Jr. (1998, 16 July). *Expectations.* The Daily Motivator. https://greatday.com/motivate/980716.html

Prospects. (2025). *Writing a Personal Statement for your CV.* London: Prospects. https://www.prospects.ac.uk/careers-advice/cvs-and-cover-letters/writing-a-personal-statement-for-your-cv

Sterkens, P., Caers, R., De Couck, M., Van Driessche, V., Geamanu, M., & Baert, S. (2023). Costly mistakes: Why and when spelling errors in resumes jeopardise interview chances. *PLOS ONE*, 18(4), e0283280. https://doi.org/10.1371/journal.pone.0283280

Sun, B., Zhu, F., Lin, S., Sun, J., Wu, Y., & Xiao, W. (2022). How is professional identity associated with teacher career satisfaction? A cross-sectional design to test the multiple mediating roles of psychological empowerment and work engagement. *International Journal of Environmental Research and Public Health*, 19(15), 9009. https://doi.org/10.3390/ijerph19159009

Swift Scout Research Team. (2025). *The Strategic Imperative of Quantification: Leveraging Data and Metrics for Enhanced Resume Effectiveness in Modern Recruitment.* SwiftScout. https://www.swiftscout.ai/blog/academic/the-strategic-imperative-of-quantification-leveraging-data-and-metrics-for-enhanced-resume-effectiveness-in-modern-recruitment

TheLadders Eye-Tracking Study. (2012). *Recruiter Review Times: How Recruiters Scan Resumes.* New York: TheLadders. Unpublished eye-tracking research report.

Worth, J., & Faulkner-Ellis, H. (2024). *Teacher labour market in England annual report 2024.* Slough, UK: National Foundation for Educational Research.

5 Mind, Motivation and Momentum

5.1 Embracing Vulnerability

You might look at the title of this chapter and feel tempted to skip it. If that's your first impulse, I encourage you to at least read the opening section. Don't worry, I'll let you know when you can stop. But before you do, I'll ask you to reflect on why your initial instinct was to turn away.

About 20 years prior to the publication of this book, my father asked me a question I thought was rather odd: 'Are you happy?'

At the time, the answer seemed obvious. Of course, I was happy. Why would he even ask? I replied with a confident 'Yes', only for him to say, 'Read *The 7 Habits of Highly Effective People* and then tell me if you change your mind'.

I hated it when my father was right. So, determined to prove him wrong, I bought the book and started reading. By the time I reached Chapter 2, I realised, much to my frustration, that he was, as usual, right.

So now I'll ask you the same question: *Are you happy?*

For many temporary teachers, the honest answer, drawn from countless first-hand accounts I've heard, is 'No'. For some of you, that may even be the reason you bought this book, turning straight to this chapter instead of one of the more practical ones.

But there will also be those who say 'Yes'. If that's you, then keep reading. Perhaps, like me, you'll reach a point where you start to wonder, frustratingly, whether the answer is as simple as you first thought.

When I first set out to write this chapter, I felt a little lost. My research led me down many paths. I read widely, explored countless books and still wondered: How do I begin?

The answer came when I returned to a passage in *Daring Greatly*. Brené Brown (2012) writes, '**we must dare to show up and let ourselves be seen**. This is vulnerability. This is *daring greatly*' (p. 2, emphasis original). That idea stayed with me as I reflected on the temporary teachers I had interviewed.

DOI: 10.4324/9781003780410-6

One story in particular kept resurfacing: A teacher arriving at a new school, unsure where to sit in the staffroom, uncertain whether anyone would even acknowledge them. At first glance, this might appear to be about loneliness, but it runs deeper than that. It is about not being seen. It is about professional identity, respect and the quiet message many temporary teachers receive that they are somehow 'less than' their permanent colleagues.

This chapter is for those temporary teachers. For anyone who has walked into a school, uncertain if their presence matters. As you read, I want you to reflect on how the ideas here can help you *dare greatly* – to show up fully, claim your professional space and be recognized and valued for the vital work you do.

As part of her research, Dr. Brené Brown divided people into two groups: those who believed they were worthy of belonging and those who did not. What she discovered intrigued me. The difference wasn't explained by obvious factors such as childhood trauma, addiction or depression. Instead, she identified two key distinctions.

1. Those who felt worthy of belonging had developed daily practices that helped them hold on to that belief.
2. They embraced vulnerability, not as a weakness, but as a catalyst for connection and growth.

They believed their vulnerabilities made them beautiful.

I'll admit, I was pessimistic at first. In the preface of her book, Dr. Brown references a viral TED Talk she gave, so I paused my reading and went in search of the video. I felt the need to scrutinise her. Despite her six *New York Times* bestsellers, I wanted to be sure this person had real credibility. If I'm honest, what I really wanted was to find a reason to discredit her. *How dare she suggest vulnerability is beautiful?* What a ridiculous statement, I thought.

As it turns out, she once felt the same way. Like any good researcher, she didn't begin with a conclusion and then look for evidence to support it. Instead, the evidence led her somewhere uncomfortable. Her own visceral reaction to the idea of showing vulnerability mirrored mine. She didn't want to discover that some people actually leaned into their vulnerability, because that meant she, a practical, scientific person, would have to consider doing the same.

If you are unsure on your relationship with vulnerability, consider the following four questions:

- *Holding back 'I love you'*: Avoiding saying 'I love you' first in a relationship, even when you feel it, because you fear rejection or that the other person won't say it back.
- *Not asking for emotional support*: Struggling silently during a tough time (such as grief, stress or anxiety) instead of opening up to a close friend or family member.

- *Pretending everything is fine*: Putting on a brave face at a family gathering or with friends, even when you're deeply unhappy, because you don't want to seem weak.
- *Hiding your passions or dreams*: Keeping quiet about something you really want to do, such as changing your career, writing a book or pursuing a hobby, because you fear people will laugh or think you're unrealistic.

For those of you feeling reluctant to read this chapter, if the answer to any of the questions is yes, it may indicate, as it did for both Dr. Brown and me, that you are nervous about how others might react when you share your vulnerability. If that's the case, I recommend you keep reading.

If you're still on the fence, I have one final plea: Consider my own vulnerability so far. If I want to write a book about flourishing as a temporary teacher, I need to be willing to *dare greatly*. That means leaning into my own vulnerabilities and seeing them not as problems to hide, but as part of the solution. Some of the stories I have shared in this book have been very intentional leading to this point. I started the preface by sharing the blind spots I had developed as a senior leader and discussed my ignorance of the challenges of supply. In the Introduction to this book, I shared a heartwarming case study from Adam Kohlbeck, who struggled as an early career teacher before supply teaching gave him the confidence to apply for a full-time post. When we consider our own vulnerability, we see them as a flaw, as a weakness, which is why we often keep them to ourselves. When you read Adam's story, in which he exposed his vulnerabilities, was your reaction to laugh and snigger at his incompetence? I believe that you didn't – that you saw it as a sign of strength and perhaps even thought of Adam as a role model. I have shared my own vulnerabilities in this book to build a trust with you, the reader, so that when you get to this final chapter, you are willing to look behind the curtain and challenge some of your thoughts that are locked up. I challenge you to dare greatly!

So why is ignoring vulnerability so harmful? Surely we could just put it in a box and lock it away. Unfortunately, it doesn't work that way. We can't numb vulnerability without also numbing joy.

Earlier in my career, my wife would often ask me how my day had been. My usual response was, 'I don't want to talk about it'. That wasn't entirely true. I didn't want to talk about the parts I found difficult – the imperfections, the mistakes I made, the child who made me feel worthless. Yet I knew that even if I wanted to share the positive moments – the child who held the door open, the student who thanked me for the lesson – I couldn't separate them from the harder parts. Any conversation about the joys of my day would inevitably lead back to the moments I didn't want to discuss. So, it was easier to say nothing at all.

And there lies the numbing of joy. The parts of my job I loved became tangled up with the parts that brought shame, and in avoiding the difficult moments, I diminished the good ones too.

Vulnerability

The *Oxford Advanced Learner's Dictionary* defines vulnerability, in an emotional context, as 'the condition of being open to emotional hurt or criticism' (Oxford University Press, 2024). No wonder many people perceive it as a weakness. However, Dr. Brown (2012, p. 34) offers a different perspective: 'I define vulnerability as uncertainty, risk, and emotional exposure'.

I experienced this firsthand when my wife was in labour with our first daughter. The doctors informed us that she needed an emergency C-section. We had been in the hospital for nearly 24 hours, and throughout the entire experience, my focus was on supporting my wife. Then, in the moment they took her away to prepare for surgery, a doctor led me to a room to put on a gown.

In that instant, I ran to the toilet and was sick. The thought of meeting my daughter for the first time, knowing the immense responsibility and the unknown ahead was terrifying. I had never felt so vulnerable. I knew I would love this child no matter what, yet I felt uncertain and exposed. The risks had never felt so real: *What if I make mistakes? What if she hates me?*

And yet, in that moment of profound vulnerability, I experienced one of the greatest days of my life.

I could write an entire book on how becoming a father has changed me for the better. In fact, it would be fair to say that making the brave decision to bring another person into the world despite the uncertainty, risks and emotional exposure was the best decision I have ever made.

Just as leaning into vulnerability can transform your personal life, it can be a powerful catalyst in your professional life. For temporary teachers, embracing vulnerability might feel uncomfortable or risky, but it is precisely this openness that allows trust, connection and growth to flourish. In the sections that follow, we will explore practical ways to lean into vulnerability at work, how to ask for support, navigate unfamiliar environments and engage authentically with students and colleagues so that uncertainty and emotional exposure become opportunities rather than obstacles.

When I asked temporary teachers to tell me when they felt most vulnerable, I received a wide range of responses:

- The moment I get the call to go to a new school.
- When I arrive and sit in the waiting area.
- Having to ask another teacher for directions.
- When a new class walks in.
- When I'm sitting in the staff room on my own
- When a student talks over my instructions.
- When I try a new teaching technique.

- When it's clear the lesson plan will not last the whole lesson.
- When a student misbehaves.
- When I need to call a member of staff to remove a student.

Do these sound like weaknesses? To me, they look like showing up, being courageous, having high expectations, challenging poor social norms.

I didn't ask the temporary teachers I interviewed how these moments made them feel, but Dr. Brown did in her studies. The responses varied, but the one that best encapsulates the experience for me was this: 'Vulnerability is like being naked onstage and hoping for applause rather than laughter' (Brown, 2012, p. 39).

It's a tough ask, to expect temporary teachers to place themselves in that position day after day. But what happens if we choose to step away from these vulnerable moments? The cost is high: Students get away with poor behaviour, lessons fall short of their potential and, in the worst cases, we stop showing up altogether. In these instances, showing up in vulnerable moments is not a sign of weakness; it is a sign of courage and strength.

It's ironic how we often see vulnerability in ourselves as weakness, yet admire it as courage in others. One powerful example comes from research into what psychologists call the *bystander effect*.

In the 1960s, social psychologists John Darley and Bibb Latané ran a now-famous experiment. They asked participants to sit alone in a room and fill out a questionnaire. Without warning, smoke began to fill the room through a vent. When someone was alone, most people reported the smoke quickly. But when participants were placed in a group, people hesitated, often looking to others to decide whether it was serious. Many stayed put, coughing and squinting, until the experimenters intervened (Darley & Latané, 1968). The conclusion showed that when we feel exposed and uncertain, we tend to freeze, waiting for someone else to take the risk of acting. It feels safer to blend in than to stand out.

Yet think of the person who does step forward – the one who waves their hand, speaks up, or runs for help. They are the one we admire. They are the one who saves the day. Their willingness to be different, to risk looking foolish or overreacting, is what transforms them into the hero of the story.

If we, as temporary teachers, can begin to reframe the emotions attached to vulnerability, shifting from feeling exposed or 'naked' to feeling proud of what we achieved, then, perhaps, when we get home and someone asks how our day went, we will feel excited to share our experiences rather than be hesitant to speak about them.

5.2 The Quiet Voice That Holds Us Back

Brown (2012) argues that vulnerability is not a weakness but the birthplace of courage, connection and growth, positioning it as a necessary condition for meaningful personal and professional development. Yet what often gets lost in how her work is interpreted is that vulnerability does not exist in isolation. We cannot lean into vulnerability without first confronting the thing that most powerfully blocks it – shame. Shame is the fear of being exposed as inadequate, unworthy or not good enough. For temporary teachers, it can sound like 'I'm just a supply', 'I don't really belong here', or 'They'll see I'm not good enough'. These thoughts do not make us weak, but they do make us hide. And when we hide, we stop taking the very risks that lead to growth, connection and wellbeing. Learning to be vulnerable, then, is not simply about being open; it is about recognising shame when it appears and choosing not to let it dictate our behaviour.

If shame is what blocks vulnerability, then learning to recognise and respond to it is one of the most important wellbeing skills a temporary teacher can develop. The good news is that shame is not something we have to simply endure. Brown's work offers a practical, evidence-based way to weaken its grip. What follows are simple strategies you can use when shame shows up in your thoughts, your body or your behaviour.

1. *Recognise and name shame*: The first step is to notice when shame is happening, as it thrives in secrecy and silence. Naming it by literally saying, 'This is shame I'm feeling' weakens its grip.
2. *Reality-check the story you're telling yourself*: Shame often feeds on distorted thoughts – 'I'm not good enough', or 'Everyone will think I'm a failure'. We can challenge those thoughts by asking: *Is this really true? What evidence do I have?*
3. *Reach out and talk about it*: Shame shrinks when we share it with someone we trust. Finding a safe listener who responds with empathy helps us see we are not alone.
4. *Practice self-compassion*: Treat yourself the way you'd treat a close friend in the same situation. Instead of self-criticism, practice kindness and remind yourself that imperfection is part of being human.

Let's look at a practical example. One experience of shame I remember vividly was when I first moved to the United States at age 15. I would walk into the dining room at lunchtime, hoping to see a familiar face from a morning lesson. Sometimes there were a few, but no one looked back at me. I silently hoped someone would wave or call me over, but no one did. I ended up sitting alone at the end of a table, day after day, until eventually I asked my mother for a packed lunch so I could eat in the restroom by myself. This sense of exclusion and isolation contributed to ongoing unhappiness and even physical illness, until I eventually moved back to the UK to live with my grandparents, a decision that had lasting consequences for my family, which we are still feeling today.

Looking back now, I wish I had understood what I know today: Shame is not your fault. Feeling excluded or judged does not make you inadequate. Recognising this is the first step toward leaning into vulnerability, building resilience and giving yourself permission to connect, even when it feels risky.

Compare this to now. When I walk into a staffroom, I sometimes get flashbacks of my American high school experience. No one looks at me. I might catch the eye of a senior leader who helped remove a student from my classroom, or the head of department who handed me some worksheets that morning, but they don't call me over.

In these moments, it's easy to feel insignificant. But after my initial anxiety kicks in, I try to take a more rational view. I have been the senior leader removing students from temporary teachers' classrooms. When I saw them in the staffroom at lunchtime, did I ignore them because they weren't important? Of course not. I was stressed, trying to juggle several challenging issues at once. In hindsight, not saying hello reflected my own workload pressures, not the worth of the temporary teacher.

The same goes for other staff who might appear to ignore a temporary teacher. Many teachers operate in survival mode. When they enter the staffroom, they gravitate toward the one or two colleagues they feel closest to. They may be practising what I describe as stage three of addressing shame: reaching out and sharing a challenging story about their morning with the people they trust, and not including a stranger.

Earlier in the book, I shared the story of the man on the subway with unruly children, whose mother had just died. That story highlights an important point: Focus on what you can control. You have no way of knowing why staff in a staffroom behave a certain way. Jumping to the conclusion that you are insignificant is understandable, but it is not logical.

If you have your own blind spots and can't move past the initial shame, this is where opening up and sharing with others becomes so important. Be prepared to listen, and don't get defensive if they don't immediately help you process your feelings. I am so appreciative of the temporary teachers I spoke to who shared their moments of shame; in doing so, they were brave and gave me the motivation to write this chapter.

There are days when my tools to support others are spent. I will discuss this more in the next section. But when I do have energy left to help, I always go out of my way to support other temporary teachers, to help them not feel alone. As I write this chapter, I am preparing to start a new role back in school leadership after a year as a temporary teacher. One thing is certain: I will make sure I practise self-compassion and treat temporary teachers with the same professional courtesy I offer all other staff I interact with in education.

To summarise, shame is uncomfortable, and it can be powerful, but it does not define you. The moments when you feel overlooked, excluded or judged are often a reflection of circumstances beyond your control, not a measure of your worth or competence. By recognising these feelings, reality-checking the stories you tell yourself, reaching out when possible and practising self-compassion, you begin to reclaim the space in which you can teach and connect confidently.

For temporary teachers, this is especially important. The very nature of temporary work exposes you to uncertainty, unfamiliar staffrooms and moments of invisibility. But leaning into vulnerability allows you to navigate those challenges without internalising them as personal failure.

5.3 Burnout

The term *burnout* was first coined by Herbert Freudenberger in the 1970s to describe a state of physical and emotional depletion resulting from prolonged stress, particularly in caring professions (Freudenberger, 1975). While burnout has several dimensions, two are especially relevant for temporary teachers: emotional exhaustion, the fatigue that comes from caring too much for too long; and a decreased sense of accomplishment, characterised by a persistent feeling that one's efforts make little difference (Freudenberger, 1975; Maslach & Jackson, 1981).

So far, we've considered a decreased sense of accomplishment through the lens of vulnerability, the stories we tell ourselves about not being good enough. But what if it's more than that? Yes, there are strategies to quiet those inner voices, but the noise may be amplified if we fail to look after ourselves, or if we don't recognise the warning signs of burnout.

Many of the temporary teachers I interviewed began their careers in permanent posts before choosing to move into supply work. The majority cited stress and anxiety as part of the reason for that shift. In fact, a 2024 Department for Education survey found that 57% of temporary teachers named high workload, stress or poor wellbeing as a reason for leaving permanent work, with 28% citing poor mental or physical health. (Department for Education, 2024).

This raises a question: *What if the problem wasn't the job itself, but rather not having the right tools to protect mental health?* Without a toolkit for managing stress, it becomes all too easy for negative feelings and low self-worth to take over.

The same DfE survey also revealed that nearly half (47%) of supply teachers wanted to leave within the next year. Of these, the reasons were almost evenly split: Some pointed to concerns about mental health and workload, while others hoped to return to a permanent position.

To both groups, I hope this section offers some reassurance. My aim is to help temporary teachers identify the signs of burnout early, and to share coping mechanisms that allow them to continue the vital work they do. And for those considering a return to permanent teaching, the goal is to equip them with the tools and mindset needed to achieve the balance they may not have found the first time around.

So what is emotional exhaustion? Maslach and Jackson (1981) define it as 'feelings of being emotionally overextended and depleted of one's emotional resources', identifying it as a core component of burnout. Put more simply, it occurs when emotional output continually exceeds emotional input – when you are giving more than you are able to replenish.

When we step back, it's no surprise that burnout is so common in education. The exact figures may vary, but the research is clear: Educators consistently report some of the highest levels of burnout of any profession. The only field with similarly high rates is medicine. What do these groups have in common? Their primary purpose is to help others. Day after day, they are faced with people in need, and the emotional investment this requires is immense. Without balancing that investment with time and care for themselves, exhaustion becomes almost inevitable.

If emotional exhaustion is the feeling of being drained, stress is often the fuel that drives it. Every time we respond to demands, whether managing a challenging class, adapting to a last-minute cover or navigating unfamiliar routines, our bodies and minds generate a stress response. That repeated stress steadily depletes our emotional resources, turning caring and effort into fatigue, and eventually leading to the emotional exhaustion we've been exploring.

This concept isn't new. In the 1930s, endocrinologist Hans Selye conducted experiments with rats at McGill University in Montreal to understand how the body responds to stress. (Selye, 1936). He exposed the rats to various stressors, heat, cold, and physical restraint and observed a series of physiological changes. Regardless of the stressor, the rats exhibited similar responses – enlarged adrenal glands, shrunken lymphatic tissues and gastric ulcers. These consistent reactions led Selye to propose the General Adaptation Syndrome (GAS), a model describing the body's three-stage response to stress:

1. *Alarm reaction*: The initial 'fight-or-flight' response, where the body prepares to confront the stressor.
2. *Resistance*: The body attempts to adapt to the ongoing stressor, maintaining a heightened state of alertness.
3. *Exhaustion*: Prolonged exposure to stress depletes the body's resources, leading to decreased function and increased vulnerability to illness.

Selye's work highlighted that stress isn't merely a psychological experience but a physiological one that can have profound effects on health. For educators, especially those in temporary roles, the constant demands and uncertainties can trigger this stress response repeatedly. Over time, without adequate recovery, this cycle can lead to the emotional exhaustion that many in the profession experience.

Cohen, Kessler and Gordon's 1995 work, *Measuring Stress: A Guide for Health and Social Scientists*, delves into the multifaceted impacts of chronic stress on health. They highlight that stress isn't merely a transient experience; prolonged exposure to stressors such as ongoing work pressures or persistent social challenges can lead to significant physiological and psychological consequences. For instance, chronic stress has been linked to compromised immune function, making individuals more susceptible to infections. Additionally, it can elevate the risk of cardiovascular diseases, including hypertension and heart disease. Psychologically, sustained stress is associated with mood disorders, anxiety and depression (Cohen, Kessler & Gordon, 1995).

In conclusion, taking care of our mental health is essential. Gone are the days when people simply shrugged their shoulders and said, 'It is what it is; you have to do what you have to do'. As educators, our roles demand a significant emotional investment. If we don't balance this output with proper self-care, we won't just experience the immediate signs of stress, sweaty palms, racing heart or tense muscles, but over time, this imbalance can take a serious toll on our overall health and wellbeing.

The first step to tackling this is to understand the stress cycle.

Mr. Patel and Ms. Jones both start their day as temporary teachers in schools they've never taught before. As students notice a new face, whispers start and a few phones sneak out. Mr. Patel feels his heart race, his palms sweat and tension knotting in his shoulders. He starts giving instructions faster and louder, hoping to regain control, but the students respond with even more chatter. His frustration grows, and by the end of the lesson, he feels exhausted and emotionally drained. This is the stress cycle in action: A stressor triggers a physiological and emotional response, which feeds back into thoughts and behaviour, intensifying the stress.

Ms. Jones faces the same challenge, but she reacts differently. When her heartbeat quickens and tension rises, she pauses, takes a deep breath and silently counts to five. She reminds herself, 'I've dealt with this before, and I can handle it'. She calls a student over to help hand out materials, subtly redirecting attention while regaining control without escalating tension. By the end of her lesson, she feels tired but accomplished, not drained. She has interrupted the stress cycle by acknowledging the stressor, regulating her physiological response and taking intentional, constructive actions, protecting her emotional energy and reducing the risk of burnout.

Stress doesn't always reveal itself immediately. Often, educators manage to keep calm and professional in the classroom, suppressing the physiological arousal and emotional tension caused by the stressor. However, once the immediate pressure is gone, the built-up stress can surface in other areas of life. For example, a teacher might deliver a lesson with composure, handling challenging students with patience; but later that evening at home, they find themselves snapping over small irritations – a forgotten cup, a text message or minor noise. This delayed response shows that stress can accumulate silently, only appearing once the urgent demands have passed, highlighting the importance of building recovery strategies to release tension before it affects other parts of life.

Continuing the theme of vulnerability, the previous example is something I can relate to. Most people I've worked with would say I'm calm under pressure, and that's true in my professional life. But it's a façade; I'm not immune to negative emotions, and it's in my personal life that my struggles with stress are more visible. I do have coping mechanisms: Exercise is a big one, and I love playing sport. Yet, the hour or two between getting home and heading out for tennis or padel is when I'm most likely to get agitated by minor things. Several mugs left scattered around the house on my wife's day off, for example, can make me feel frustrated at 5 p.m., but by 8 p.m., after exercise, I barely even notice them. I share this story to highlight, once again, our mixed responses to vulnerability. Admitting that you snap over small, irrelevant things can feel like a sign of weakness. Yet, perhaps as you read these words, you sensed that I, as the author, was being brave in sharing my daily struggles.

Research consistently shows that exercise can be a powerful tool in managing stress. For example, Salmon (2001) found that both aerobic and resistance exercise help reduce anxiety, depression and sensitivity to stress. Exercise works on multiple levels: It lowers stress hormones such as cortisol and adrenaline while boosting endorphins, the body's natural 'feel-good' chemicals. This combination not only helps alleviate immediate feelings of tension but also strengthens resilience, making it easier to cope with daily stressors.

But most readers already know that exercise helps. The real challenge isn't identifying what reduces stress; it's actually making the time and commitment to do it.

I wrote at the beginning of this chapter the disagreement I had with my father about my happiness, where he suggested I read *The 7 Habits of Highly Effective People* (Covey, 1989) before jumping to conclusions. This book had a profound effect on me and led me to become obsessed with the concept of habits, so much so that I named my first book *Learning Habits*.

The epiphany I had linked directly to Stephen Covey's second habit, 'Begin with the End in Mind'. He illustrates this with the story of a jar being filled with rocks, pebbles and sand. The rocks represent the most important priorities in life – family, health, personal goals. The pebbles are things that matter but are less critical, and the sand represents the small, trivial tasks. If you fill the jar with sand first, there's no room for the rocks or pebbles. But if you place the rocks first, then the pebbles, then the sand, everything fits.

This metaphor made me realise how my own life had become unbalanced. I was obsessed with my job, pouring endless hours into teaching, day and night. The book forced me to reflect on my 'rocks' – what truly mattered to me. I had a Eureka moment: Before becoming a teacher, I used to play rugby, and I was pretty good. I had loved the thrill of scoring a try, the camaraderie with friends, the discussions about the game. But over time, all of that had vanished as I chased the ideal of the 'perfect teacher'.

My father was right; I was unhappy. I had tricked myself with this new identity. Not only had I squeezed out a part of life I loved, but I had also lost the very outlet that helped me manage daily stress. By defining myself solely as a teacher, my happiness became entirely dependent on my work. On a bad day at school, it felt as if my whole life had failed because the one thing I had set out to do, I had defined myself by it I couldn't get right.

Covey's solution was to identify the 'sand' – the trivial, time-wasting things in my life. I made a list and quickly realised it all boiled down to procrastination. The hours I spent scrolling on my phone, watching TV shows I wasn't even invested in or buying material items that brought no real satisfaction added up to far more time than I needed to return to playing rugby. Once I recognised this, I made a conscious choice: I reclaimed that time and started playing again.

5.4 Happiness

For me, at the time, it was simple: Sport made me happy. It gave me the energy I needed to recharge my emotional batteries. Now, as I write this book and reflect on that decision, I can't help but wonder: What would my life have been like if I hadn't chosen to play sport again? What if I had continued down the path of total commitment to my job, pushing aside everything else?

Looking back on more than 20 years in education, I can say with confidence that my career has been successful. I led a science department in one of the most successful comprehensive schools in the country, then became a senior leader in a prestigious Catholic school. Eventually, I stepped away to take up supply teaching and write an educational book, a decision that, coincidentally, brought me to this second book, the one you are now reading.

When I first read *The Happiness Advantage* by Achor (2010), I felt both frustrated and enlightened. Frustrated, because it confirmed what my father had been telling me all along: Not only was I unhappy at the time, but happiness itself is a driving force behind success. As Achor's (2010) research shows, we don't become happy because we are successful; rather, we become more successful when we are happier and more positive.

Achor begins his book by sharing research from Harvard University, where he found that 80% of students reported being unhappy. In a strange way, that gave me comfort; after all, before my father's intervention, my own unhappiness was in line with students at one of the most prestigious institutions in the world. The real revelation, though, is in the evidence Achor presents about the power of positivity: people who are happier make better decisions. For instance, doctors put into a positive mood before making a diagnosis demonstrated nearly three times more intelligence and creativity than doctors in a neutral state, and they made accurate diagnoses 19% faster.

This made me reflect on my own career. Perhaps the successes I've achieved were not completely due to my commitment as an educator, but also in part to my general happiness. In fact, a helpful summary from the British Psychological Society's blog explains that after reviewing 225 studies involving more than 275,000 people, Lyubomirsky and colleagues concluded that happiness doesn't just follow success, it often causes it. (Lyubomirsky, King & Diener, 2005). Happier individuals tend to have better relationships, more fulfilling work and healthier lives, and in many cases happiness actually precedes those outcomes. Seen in this light, my father's words echo even louder. Happiness wasn't simply a personal comfort; it may well have been a professional advantage, shaping the trajectory of my career in ways I hadn't fully appreciated until now.

When I first set out to write this chapter, my goal was simple: To support the mental health of temporary teachers. My hope now is that by helping temporary teachers find the things that genuinely make them happy, they will not only recharge their emotional batteries and avoid burnout, but also unlock a more successful and fulfilling professional life.

I want to be clear about what I mean here. As a temporary teacher, the only person you truly need to justify your work to is yourself. Throughout this book, I have suggested strategies you can use to support students' learning, even in the challenging and unpredictable environments you often find yourself in. These ideas are not quick fixes; they are not a magic wand that you can wave and see instant results. They require time, patience and motivation.

And this is where happiness plays such an important role. If you are unhappy, trying to implement new approaches can feel almost impossible. On the other hand, if you invest in your wellbeing and walk into schools with a smile, these strategies become easier to apply. More than that, the small successes you achieve can bring a sense of satisfaction that may have been missing before.

Ultimately, my hope is that this shift allows you to see yourself differently, not as 'just a supply or substitute teacher', but as a temporary teacher who makes a positive impact on the lives of those around you. When you reach that point, the opinions and noise of others begin to matter far less, because you'll know the value you bring.

The good news is that happiness doesn't come from one source alone. Researchers suggest that while genetics play a role in setting our baseline (Lykken & Tellegen, 1996), much of our day-to-day happiness comes from the choices we make and the relationships we build. Sonja Lyubomirsky et al. (2005) argue that only around 10% of happiness is shaped by life circumstances such as income, status or possessions, while as much as 40% can be influenced by intentional activities – the things we do deliberately – such as practicing gratitude, exercising or nurturing relationships.

Long-running studies also show that relationships are central to wellbeing. The Harvard Study of Adult Development, which has tracked participants for over 80 years, found that close social connections, not wealth or fame, were the strongest predictors of happiness and long-term health (Vaillant, 2012).

Before we turn to the final section, pause and give yourself space to reflect on what truly makes you happy outside of your teaching role. Use the prompts that follow to explore your energy, priorities and sources of fulfilment.

Where Does Your Happiness Come From?

Energy and Enjoyment

- When in the last month did you feel most alive or excited outside of work? What were you doing, and who was with you?
- What hobbies, activities or experiences consistently lift your mood?
- If you had an extra hour each day, what would you spend it on to feel more fulfilled?

Relationships and Social Connection

- Which relationships outside of work give you the most support and joy? How can you invest in them this week?
- Who makes you laugh, feel understood or energised? How can you spend more time with them?
- Are there friendships or family connections you've neglected that you could reconnect with?

Mindset and Perspective

- What personal beliefs or stories about yourself limit your happiness? How could you reframe them positively?
- When was the last time you felt proud of something outside school? What does that tell you about your values and strengths?

Positive Focus and Gratitude

- What three non-work moments this week brought you genuine satisfaction or contentment?
- Which small pleasures do you tend to overlook – your morning coffee, a walk, music, exercise? How can you make more space for them?

Growth and Challenge

- What non-work goal or personal project excites you right now? How can you make small steps toward it this week?
- Have recent challenges outside of school taught you something valuable about yourself?

Meaning and Purpose

- When you look back on the past month, what moments outside work made life feel meaningful?
- If you could dedicate more time to one thing that aligns with your values, what would it be and why?

5.5 Reclaiming Your Energy

Before you start building new habits, there's a step that often goes unnoticed. It's the pause before the plan, the moment where you check in with yourself, not as a professional trying to improve, but as a person trying to reconnect.

We often rush to change our behaviour without first tending to the mindset and emotional energy behind it. We set goals, buy planners and create routines; yet if we haven't renewed our sense of self-worth, those systems rarely last. The foundation for any lasting habit isn't motivation; it's self-respect. This section is about that foundation, the quiet, inner work of reclaiming your energy.

The Inner Foundation

The first book I ever read about wellbeing was by Vex King (2018). What really struck a chord with me in his work wasn't just his ideas, but his story.

King's story is one of transformation. He grew up in hardship, poverty, discrimination and loss, in circumstances that could easily have defined his future. As a young man, he carried the weight of anger and frustration, not because he lacked ambition, but because the world around him seemed to offer little hope. Life was about surviving the next challenge, not dreaming of something better.

He speaks candidly about the years he spent in what he called *survival mode*, constantly alert, guarded and reactive. It's a state many of us drift into at times, even without realising it: Moving through our days with a low hum of stress, always managing, always coping, but rarely pausing to ask what all that effort is for.

His turning point came when he began to challenge the stories he told himself about who he was and what he deserved. He realised that waiting for the world to change wasn't working. So he began to change the way he responded to it. That shift wasn't dramatic or glamorous. Rather, it started with a single, radical idea – *self-love*. Not the superficial kind that gets reduced to slogans or self-care hashtags, but the grounded kind that begins with *self-respect*, the quiet, consistent belief that your time, energy and wellbeing matter.

What resonated with me most was how practical that sounded. It wasn't about detaching from reality or pretending everything was fine. It was about acknowledging pain, frustration and fatigue and then choosing not to let them define you. It was about turning compassion inward, especially in moments when the instinct is to criticise or compare.

That message has real weight for temporary teachers. When you're moving from one school to another, adapting to new systems and often feeling like a guest in someone else's space, it's easy to lose that sense of rootedness. You give so much of your energy, patience and professionalism, often without the consistency or community that permanent roles can offer.

In that context, reclaiming your energy becomes more than a wellbeing practice; it's an act of survival. It means reminding yourself that your worth isn't defined by a single day, a single class or how you're perceived by a staffroom you might never see again. It means recognising that every school you step into benefits from your flexibility, your adaptability and your professionalism.

Reclaiming your energy begins there, not with strategies or routines, but with a renewed understanding that you are allowed to value yourself, even in the chaos.

It's about building a mindset that travels with you, one that supports who you are, not just what you do.

The energy we carry shapes the spaces we enter. Students, colleagues and even strangers pick up on it, often subconsciously. If you walk into a classroom carrying the residue of stress or self-doubt, that energy subtly spreads. Equally, when you arrive calm, composed and open, the atmosphere follows.

That doesn't mean forcing positivity or pretending everything is fine. It means taking a moment to centre yourself before you step into the room, a deep breath, a silent reminder or even a short ritual that helps you arrive fully. These small acts are not about performance; they're about presence.

Teaching is emotional work. Every interaction transmits something. Protecting and replenishing your energy allows you to transmit the right things – patience, empathy, curiosity – consistently and sustainably.

One of the quietest forms of self-love is choosing response over reaction. When we react, we give away control. When we respond, we take it back. A difficult class, an unexpected timetable change, an offhand comment from a colleague – these moments can trigger frustration or defensiveness. But between the event and your response, there's a small gap. That gap is where agency lives.

Protecting that space is an act of care. It gives you room to breathe, to choose calm over chaos. Over time, this ability to pause and respond doesn't just change how you manage classrooms; it changes how you manage yourself.

Before building new habits, it helps to reconnect with what's already working. When life feels scattered, gratitude acts like gravity, pulling you back to what still has value.

Notice the moments that give meaning to your day:

- A student who says thank you.
- The quiet between lessons.
- The small success of adapting to a new environment.

Gratitude doesn't dismiss difficulty; it balances it. It shifts your focus from what's missing to what's present, and from what's draining to what's sustaining. It's hard to build meaningful habits if you're operating from scarcity. Gratitude helps you remember that you're already standing on something solid.

Reclaiming your energy isn't about becoming a new person. It's about reconnecting with the parts of you that the demands of temporary teaching may have dulled – curiosity, compassion, humour and calm.

Before you start designing new routines or changing your habits, make space to listen to yourself. Ask:

- What kind of life do I want my routines to support?
- What values do I want my actions to reflect?
- What makes me feel most like *me*?

The answers to these questions form the emotional scaffolding for every habit you'll build later. Without them, habits become hollow, mechanical responses to pressure rather than expressions of who you are.

You can explore these questions in practical ways:

1. *Quick daily check-in*: Set aside five minutes at the start or end of your day to check in with yourself. Ask:

   How am I feeling physically, emotionally and mentally?

   Which moments today aligned with my values?

   Where did I act out of obligation rather than intention?

Record one small observation in a notebook or journal. Over time, these snapshots reveal patterns about what energises you and what drains you.

2. *Self-love rituals*: Self-love doesn't have to be complicated. Small, consistent rituals reinforce the idea that your energy matters. Examples include:

   A short morning affirmation, such as, 'I bring patience, calm, and energy into this day, and I am enough as I am'.

   Blocking a ten-minute pause in your day to breathe, stretch or simply notice your surroundings.

   Giving yourself permission to leave the school site without guilt when your work is done, rather than lingering out of obligation.

3. *Celebrate small wins*: Temporary teaching often means small successes go unnoticed. Take a moment to acknowledge them:

   A lesson that went better than expected.

   A student who engaged or thanked you.

   Adapting to a new school environment successfully.

Write down at least one win each day. This builds a habit of noticing your own contribution and reinforces self-respect.

4. *Energy audit*: Spend a few minutes reflecting weekly:

   Which activities, tasks or people energised me?

   Which drained me unnecessarily?

   How can I protect my energy and prioritise what restores me?

This helps you make intentional choices about where to invest your time and emotional energy, reinforcing that your wellbeing is a priority.

5. *Micro-decisions of self-respect*: Self-love often shows up in small, practical choices:

   Saying 'no' politely but firmly to extra work when your capacity is full.

   Taking a lunch break away from your desk or staffroom.

   Choosing a task that gives you satisfaction, even if it feels minor.

These micro-decisions reinforce that your time, energy and wellbeing matter, and they accumulate into a stronger, more resilient mindset.

Reclaiming your energy is not about slowing down; it's about tuning in. It's choosing to act from self-respect rather than self-criticism, to lead your day rather than be led by it.

Before you decide what changes to make next, take a moment to remember this: You are not a project to fix; you are a person to care for. And from that place of care, real and lasting change begins.

5.6 Forming New Habits

I have discussed at length how *The 7 Habits of Highly Effective People* served as a valuable wake-up call, helping me shake off my slumber. However, putting these habits into practice hasn't been easy. I've stumbled and fallen off the wagon many times, and here's why.

Habits

A habit is a behaviour or action that we perform automatically, often without conscious thought, because it has been repeated frequently enough to become ingrained in our routines. Habits form through a process in the brain called the habit loop, which has three parts – a cue that triggers the behaviour, the routine itself and a reward that reinforces it. Over time, this loop becomes so automatic that the behaviour can occur almost reflexively, making habits powerful drivers of both positive and negative aspects of our lives. In other words, habits are the invisible architecture of daily life. They shape what we do, how we feel, and often how successful or stressed we are, without us even realizing it.

For temporary teachers, much of what we do in the classroom becomes habitual – how we give instructions , interact with students or react to challenging situations. Positive habits, like setting aside time for exercise or reflection, can help replenish our emotional resources and buffer against stress. Negative habits, such as skipping breaks, overworking or ruminating on mistakes, silently fuel emotional exhaustion and burnout. Because habits operate automatically, they can either protect our wellbeing or undermine it, often without our noticing until the effects are clear. Understanding and intentionally shaping our habits is therefore a crucial step in managing stress and sustaining ourselves in the high-demand world of education.

Forming Habits for Wellbeing

To protect your wellbeing and avoid burnout, you may need to form some new habits, or replace old ones. What this looks like will be different for everyone. For some, it might mean playing sport or exercising to relieve stress and build meaningful friendships. For others, it could be joining a book club or reading alone with a candlelit bath. You might also have tried to give up habits you know don't serve you well, like smoking, scrolling late into the night or eating too much unhealthy food.

The important thing is that there's no single right answer. Everyone's version of self-care looks different. This section focuses not on *what* habits to build, but *how* to build them effectively. Because one thing is certain: Breaking bad habits or starting new ones is hard.

Understanding the Habit Loop

Habits follow a simple but powerful cycle: *cue → routine (or response) → reward* (Clear, 2018; Duhigg, 2012).

The cue is the trigger that initiates the behaviour. Much of our daily life runs on autopilot; guided by these cues, getting home from work, opening the fridge or sitting on the sofa may all prompt familiar routines without our consciously deciding to do them.

Charles Duhigg (2012), in *The Power of Habit*, illustrates the strength of cues through the story of how brushing teeth became a national habit in the United States. In the early 1900s, only around 7% of Americans brushed their teeth daily. A marketing campaign introduced a toothpaste called Pepsodent, which used an advert showing an actor running their tongue over their teeth and talking about the 'film' they could feel. This simple physical sensation became the cue to brush, turning toothbrushing from a rare practice into a national routine within a decade.

The takeaway: No one *feels* like brushing their teeth, but the cue ('the film on your teeth') made it automatic.

Identifying Your Cues

If you want to start something new, begin by identifying your existing cues. Habits are difficult to break because their triggers are often invisible. You might find yourself doomscrolling on your phone without making a conscious decision; it's simply your brain responding to a cue, like tiredness, boredom or anxiety.

To make progress, start by *noticing* what's really happening in your day. Many of our habits run quietly in the background, so the first step is to bring them into view. One simple but powerful tool for this is the habit scorecard (Clear, 2018). Begin by writing down everything you typically do in an evening, step by step. For example:

- Get home from work.
- Get changed.
- Feed the dog.
- Go on my phone.
- Do the washing.
- Cook tea.
- Go on my phone.
- Wash the dishes.
- Go to bed.

Then, mark each action with a (+) if it supports your wellbeing or (–) if it doesn't. You might also add a (=) for neutral activities.

The goal isn't to criticise yourself, but to observe patterns and triggers. Perhaps you notice that you often reach for your phone when you're tired, or that scrolling tends to appear between other tasks. Once you can see your routine clearly, you can start to reshape it, replacing unhelpful habits with ones that serve you better.

Habit Stacking and Implementation Intentions

A common reason people give for not building new habits is *time*: 'I'd go to the gym, but I don't have the time'. Often, it's not a lack of time; it's a lack of a clear plan and cue. Two strategies that can help are habit stacking and implementation intentions.

- Habit stacking involves linking a new habit to one you already do. For example:

  After I feed the dog, I will read for 10 minutes.
  After I change out of my work clothes, I will put on my running gear.

The existing habit becomes the cue for the new one, increasing the chances you'll follow through (Clear, 2018).

- Implementation intentions take this a step further. Research by Peter Gollwitzer (1999) shows that people are significantly more likely to achieve their goals when they specify when and where they'll do them. For example, 'When I get home at 5:30, I'll go for a run in the park'.

Reward and Reinforcement

Habits stick because of rewards. Edward Thorndike's *Law of Effect* (1898) states that behaviours followed by satisfying outcomes are more likely to be repeated, while those followed by unpleasant outcomes are not. His famous experiment with cats escaping puzzle boxes showed that, over time, behaviours leading to a reward (escape and food) were repeated faster and more efficiently.

You can use this same principle to your advantage. Plan a small reward for yourself after completing a new habit, such as a bath after a jog or a favourite podcast after marking.

Neuroscience helps explain why this works. In a well-known study, neuroscientist Wolfram Schultz (1998) trained mice to press a lever to receive a drop of sweet liquid. At first, the animals' dopamine levels spiked when the liquid was delivered. But after repeated trials, something remarkable happened: The dopamine surge began *earlier* – not when the mice received the reward, but when they heard the sound that signalled it was on its way. Their brains had learned to associate the anticipation of the reward with pleasure. When the expected reward didn't arrive, dopamine levels actually fell, showing clear disappointment. Schultz concluded that dopamine doesn't just make us feel good after a reward; it motivates us to seek the reward in the first place.

This finding has powerful implications for habit formation. When you decide on a reward ahead of time, such as a relaxing bath after a run or a quiet coffee after lesson planning, your brain begins releasing dopamine *in anticipation* of that reward. That means motivation often appears before the reward itself, helping you take the first step towards the habit you want to build.

Make It Easy

Another key to making habits stick is to make them as easy as possible to start. The success of the UK's *Couch to 5K* programme demonstrates this: It begins with participants running for just one minute at a time. According to the National Health Service (NHS), over 5 million people have downloaded the app, and completion rates are among the highest of any public health initiative (NHS Digital, 2021). The reason? The first step is so small it feels impossible to fail, and once you start, momentum often carries you further.

To make your own new habits easier:

- *Prepare your environment.* Lay out your gym clothes where you'll see them when you get home. Seeing them becomes the cue that reminds you to act.
- *Hide cues for bad habits.* Leave your phone in another room if it distracts you; place a book where your phone usually sits.
- *Change your environment.* If sitting on the sofa leads to unproductive habits, take a different route home that passes the gym.

Case Study: Changing a Lunchtime Habit

After completing a habit scorecard, you notice a familiar pattern: Every lunchtime, you scroll on your phone. You hadn't planned to, but the moment you sit down in the staffroom, your hand reaches for your phone almost automatically. It's become a small act of comfort in what can sometimes feel like a lonely part of the day.

For many temporary teachers, lunchtime can be an isolating experience. You might not have a regular team to sit with, or you might be in a different school each day. In these moments, reaching for your phone provides a sense of connection and familiarity. The scrolling itself isn't the problem; it's that it's automatic, and it often leaves you feeling no better than before.

Alongside this, you've been thinking about wanting to eat more healthily. By using what you've learned about habit formation, you can turn that lunchtime scroll into something more positive.

1. *Identify the cue.* The cue for the habit is sitting down in the staffroom at lunchtime. This is when the urge to reach for your phone begins.

2. *Create a clear plan.* Instead of trying to resist your phone altogether, you decide to *redirect* the habit:

   When I pick up my phone at lunchtime, I will look at healthy meal ideas instead of scrolling social media.

   This gives your existing cue a new, more productive response.

3. *Make the new habit easier.* To make this easier to follow through, you change your phone's environment: Remove social media apps from your home screen and leave just one food-related app visible – perhaps a recipe app or a supermarket's meal planner. Now, when you pick up your phone, the first cue you see encourages the new behaviour.

4. *Change your physical environment.* To reinforce this new habit, you also adjust your route home so that it passes a supermarket. That way, when you finish work, you can quickly pick up the ingredients for the meal you planned at lunchtime. This makes the transition from intention to action almost effortless.

5. *Reward the new habit.* When you get home, you cook and enjoy the healthy meal you planned – creating a clear, satisfying reward. Over time, your brain begins to associate lunchtime planning with that sense of satisfaction and wellbeing.

Within a few weeks, your old habit of scrolling at lunchtime begins to fade. You've replaced it with something small but meaningful – one that leaves you feeling more in control, healthier, and less isolated.

This example highlights a simple truth: Changing habits doesn't always mean radical transformation. Often, it's about recognising small moments of automatic behaviour and reshaping them with clear intentions and thoughtful environmental cues.

To conclude this chapter, revisit your happiness survey on page 117 and consider how you might use the strategies suggested in this section to make the things that bring you joy a more permanent fixture in your life. To reference Stephen Covey's *The 7 Habits of Highly Effective People* one last time: Find your 'rocks' and develop strategies to turn them into daily habits. This will help reduce the possibility of burnout and give you the headspace to lean into your vulnerabilities.

References

Achor, S. (2010). *The Happiness Advantage: The Seven Principles of Positive Psychology that Fuel Success and Performance at Work*. New York: Crown Business.

Brown, B. (2012). *Daring Greatly: How the Courage to Be Vulnerable Transforms the Way We Live, Love, Parent, and Lead*. New York: Gotham Books.

Clear, J. (2018). *Atomic Habits: An Easy & Proven Way to Build Good Habits & Break Bad Ones*. London: Penguin.

Cohen, S., Kessler, R. C., & Gordon, L. U. (1995). *Measuring Stress: A Guide for Health and Social Scientists*. New York: Oxford University Press.

Covey, S. R. (1989). *The 7 habits of highly effective people: Powerful lessons in personal change*. New York: Free Press.

Darley, J. M., & Latané, B. (1968). Bystander intervention in emergencies: Diffusion of responsibility. *Journal of Personality and Social Psychology*, 8(4), 377–383. https://doi.org/10.1037/h0025589

Department for Education (DfE). (2024). *School Workforce in England: Reporting and Wellbeing Survey*. London: DfE.

Duhigg, C. (2012). *The Power of Habit: Why We Do What We Do in Life and Business*. London: Random House.

Freudenberger, H. J. (1975). The staff burn-out syndrome in alternative institutions. *Psychotherapy: Theory, Research & Practice*, 12(1), 73–82.

Gollwitzer, P. M. (1999). Implementation intentions: Strong effects of simple plans. *American Psychologist*, 54(7), 493–503. https://doi.org/10.1037/0003-066X.54.7.493

King, V. (2018). *Good Vibes, Good Life: How Self-love and Kindness Can Transform Your Life*. London: Harper Element.

Lykken, D., & Tellegen, A. (1996). Happiness is a stochastic phenomenon. *Psychological Science*, 7(3), 186–189. https://doi.org/10.1111/j.1467-9280.1996.tb00355.x

Lyubomirsky, S., King, L., & Diener, E. (2005). The benefits of frequent positive affect: Does happiness lead to success? *Psychological Bulletin*, 131(6), 803–855. https://doi.org/10.1037/0033-2909.131.6.803

Maslach, C., & Jackson, S. E. (1981). The measurement of experienced burnout. *Journal of Occupational Behavior*, 2(2), 99–113.

NHS Digital. (2021). *Couch to 5K App Usage Statistics*. NHS Digital. https://digital.nhs.uk/services/couch-to-5k

Oxford University Press. (2024). Vulnerability. In *Oxford Learner's Dictionaries*. https://www.oxfordlearnersdictionaries.com

Salmon, P. (2001). Effects of physical exercise on anxiety, depression, and sensitivity to stress: A unifying theory. *Clinical Psychology Review*, 21(1), 33–61. https://doi.org/10.1016/S0272-7358(99)00032-X

Schultz, W. (1998). Predictive reward signal of dopamine neurons. *Journal of Neurophysiology*, 80(1), 1–27. https://doi.org/10.1152/jn.1998.80.1.1

Selye, H. (1936). A syndrome produced by diverse nocuous agents. *Nature*, 138, 32.
Thorndike, E. L. (1898). *Animal Intelligence: An Experimental Study of the Associative Processes in Animals.* New York: Macmillan.
Vaillant, G. E. (2012). *Triumphs of Experience: The Men of the Harvard Grant Study.* Cambridge, MA: Belknap Press of Harvard University Press.

Conclusion

'It's just supply teaching, I'll be fine'.

Those were the words that opened this book, and in many ways, they capture the misunderstanding that surrounds temporary teaching – the idea that because something is temporary, it requires less skill, less care or less emotional investment. I believed that myself. I also believed that experience and job titles would protect me.

They didn't.

What I came to understand, both through temporary teaching and through writing this book, is that temporary teaching is not simply a role you *do*. It is something you have to *become*. Each unfamiliar classroom tests your professional identity. Each school asks you to take responsibility quickly, often without being fully welcomed into the community.

That tension – responsibility without recognition – wears people down.

Ten years ago, our daughter was born with an incurable illness that required a liver transplant. For eight months, my wife lived in the hospital with her. During that time, I stayed at a Ronald McDonald House alongside other families facing similar uncertainty. Each morning, sandwiches arrived from Pret – practical gestures that may have looked small from the outside, but which removed one worry from an already overwhelming day.

Those acts did not change our daughter's diagnosis. They did something just as important: They helped us hold on to our identity as parents when crisis threatened to reduce us to medical cases and visiting hours. They gave us a sense of belonging at a time when life felt completely unfamiliar.

Temporary teachers often need the same thing. They walk into schools carrying responsibility for learning, behaviour and safety, yet are frequently treated as peripheral. Over time, this erodes confidence and professional identity. This book exists to push back against that quiet erosion and to say clearly: The work you do matters.

DOI: 10.4324/9781003780410-7

I didn't write this book for recognition or reward. I wrote it because I wanted temporary teachers to see themselves as skilled professionals, and because I had the experience to offer something useful. Writing it has brought me an unexpected sense of happiness and clarity. In helping others make sense of uncertainty, I rebuilt confidence in my own professional identity.

There is a quiet irony there. In trying to help others belong, I strengthened my own sense of belonging.

If you have reached the end of this book, my hope is simple. That you feel less alone when you walk into an unfamiliar school. That you understand your impact more clearly. And that you recognise that belonging does not come from contracts, titles or length of service. It comes from feeling seen and valued for the work you do.

Because it was never 'just supply teaching'. And you were always more than just temporary.

Index

Pages in **bold** refer to tables, pages in **bold-*italics*** refer to boxes.

www.ingramcontent.com/pod-product-compliance
Lightning Source LLC
LaVergne TN
LVHW081738070826
845179LV00025B/340